To Jane —
Enjoy!
Bonnie

Baking Secrets

— for —

Grand Occasions & Ordinary Days

revealed by

BONNIE BAILEY

Baking Secrets
for Grand Occasions & Ordinary Days

Copyright © 2002 by Bonnie S. Bailey
127 Queensberry Crescent
Birmingham, Alabama 35223
205-970-0550

ISBN: 0-9634316-9-2

Edited, designed, and manufactured by Favorite Recipes® Press,
an imprint of

FRP

2451 Atrium Way
Nashville, Tennessee 37214
1-800-358-0560

Manufactured in the United States of America
First Printing 2002   7,500 copies

Book Design: Brad Whitfield, Susan Breining
Art Director: Steve Newman
Managing Editor: Mary Cummings
Project Editor: Judy Jackson

Artwork: Jennifer Wallace
Photography: Mac Jamieson
Stylist: Richard Joseph (Cole Lollar)

Preface

There are few, if any, "secrets" to baking; "mysteries," maybe, or "enigmas," but as King Solomon said, there really is nothing new under the sun. Those of us who are not very exacting in what we do, but who measure by "pinches" and "a bit of this and a bit of that," tend to annoy those of you who want "exactly $1/8$ teaspoon" in a recipe.

That chasm between us, I think, is what makes the world a better place. Exactness and variation in baking and dessert-making are both really necessary to an extent, and, therefore, we opposites need each other to balance out. Generally, most people find it easy to accept the exactness necessary for baking and dessert making, but don't realize how necessary it is to allow for variations. Flour that has been refrigerated will weigh more than flour that has been in a dry cabinet, because refrigerators contain a lot of moisture. Unsalted butter also contains quite a bit of water, and brands can differ greatly. Therefore, feel, smell, taste, touch, and general common sense are as important in baking and dessert making as in anything else.

When I ran a bakery in the 1980s, I always looked for a very maternal, nurturing person, whether male or female, because he or she would make the very best baker and dessert maker. Past experience made no difference in their abilities, because nurturers just cared so much! Desserts and baking take care, and some require a lot of time. Baked foods and desserts generally have to have a broad spectrum of appeal, too. Salmon, for example, is only going to appeal to a relatively small audience; whereas a birthday cake is going to have to appeal to toddlers, teens, grandparents, and all in between. Of course, each person will have her or his own imprimatur, so truly, there is nothing new under the sun. Just as all people are unique, even twins, so are the products of bakers and dessert makers. Even though we all follow the exact same recipe, we usually find that the end product can vary greatly. Mrs. Field shares her cookies, Sister Shubert shares her rolls, and so many others share their recipes because they are secure in their own uniqueness. That's another thing about bakers and dessert makers: they are usually very giving people. I guess that's why I personally love desserts and baking especially— there's so much for which to strive, and, almost always, there are such sweet people with whom to work.

Even if you have never enjoyed baking or dessert making, give some of these "secrets" a try. These are recipes and techniques that are so simple that I actually have broken all other promises to myself never to write another cookbook (I said I'd write a Western with one hero and one horse, but I never did that either). These recipes are easy and quick and safely variable. They are the ones that I use with my own grandchildren. Remember, there are no mistakes in baking, just more crumbs. May you too enjoy these "secrets" with your own cherished circle and may they continually help your circle to increase.

Dedication

To my grandchildren, Jack, Katherine, Chloe, and Anne,
because I love you very, very much

and to my sons, Charles, John, and Evans, who have always enjoyed telling
people that they are, each one, "a son of a baker"

and to my sweet friend Kris, Charles' wife, with whom I travel and learn and grow

and, of course, to Bill, who has brought more good, sweet things to our lives
than any baker or dessert maker on earth.

Table of Contents

In Gratitude

A MILLION THANKS

To my sister, Virginia Johnson, who shared many of her recipes with me for this book,
and her friendship and laughter for our whole lives.

To Edward and Virginia Matson, who saw to it that I received the Vicki Penziner Matson Award of the
Chicago Sun-Times/Friends of Literature for my first book, Remembrances of Things Passed.
I am still humbled by their work in recognizing me, and I am exceedingly grateful.

To Jennifer Wallace, the illustrator of this book, for pouring her heart into it.
It really shows, and I am amazed and grateful.

AND to all of the other good friends and helpers who are mentioned as we go through the book.
They, too, know that I am eternally grateful to every one of them for turning my
"Ordinary Days" into "Grand Occasions."

Serving breakfast every morning soon becomes unbearable to me if I have to serve sweet things all the time. This was especially true when I worked as a chef at a bed-and-breakfast. The Lodge at Gorham's Bluff, where I worked one late fall and winter, is in the foothills of the Appalachians, and, thankfully, a big hearty mountain breakfast does not depend on sugary things. I also found that almost a third of all our guests were on no-fat vegetarian diets, with little or no refined sugar. A high-end B&B like The Lodge is delighted to accommodate special needs and desires. Many of our health-conscious guests were young women who were battling or recovering from difficult bouts with breast cancer or other serious medical problems. Their friends and/or husbands had given them the weekend away, often away from little children and always from the austere hospital and clinic lives that surrounded them. Knowing that, innkeepers Dana McCarn, Miranda, and Danielle made all of us try our very best to make their stays (and that of all our guests) very special.

Egg substitutes and low-fat or no-fat dairy products actually can be excellent, but it takes some searching out to find them. Some sausages are made from chicken and apples, chicken and fennel, and all kinds of delicious and low-fat or no-fat ingredients. Labeling has made the task much easier than ever before, and it is important to know your ingredients, especially in substitutes. Some dairy substitutes especially are better than others for cooking. Very good olive oils, fresh herbs and vegetables, whole grains, whether in cereals or breads, and fresh fruit are permissible in sensible portions on almost all special diets. The things usually to be avoided are high-density fats, refined sugars, additives, and, occasionally, high-sodium foods. Some food allergies are deadly, such as to shellfish and nuts. Labeling and education and good common sense are the best guidelines.

The recipes in the first section of this book usually call for eggs, unsalted butter, and cheeses, but any and all of these can be replaced by good substitutes. Just read the labels, and try them out first for taste. You will also probably have to be very generous in "seasoning to taste" with fresh herbs, freshly ground pepper, and/or any fresh vegetables that are permissible on your diet.

Baking Savories
for Breakfasts & Brunches

Contents

Cheddar Cheese Grits

This recipe comes straight from my friend Betty Sims, who is the author of Southern Scrumptious: How to Cater Your Own Party. *Her recipe, Gruyère Cheese Grits, is on page 63 of her book. I know it by heart, because I made it almost every single morning for one entire fall and winter. I still use it for every occasion I can find for it. It's doubled here, and I have added two extra eggs and more salt and herbs, but, generally, for loose-cannon cooks like I am, it's the same as Betty's.*

My version fills a 10x15-inch baking dish and makes about 18 small servings. You can divide it exactly in half, as Betty's original recipe is, if you have a smaller crowd, but use a 2-quart or a 9x13-inch baking dish.

6 cups milk
2 cups quick-cooking (not instant) grits
1 cup (2 sticks) unsalted butter
1 tablespoon salt
2 cups cold milk
4 eggs, beaten
2 tablespoons any one or any combination of dried dill, thyme, or sage
   (if using fresh herbs, see Note)
2 cups any one or any combination of shredded Cheddar, Gruyère, or
   Swiss cheese

Bring 6 cups milk to a boil in a saucepan. Stir in the grits, butter, and salt. Cook until the mixture is thick and bubbly, stirring constantly. Add 2 cups milk, stirring to cool the mixture. Stir in the eggs, dried herbs, and half the cheese. Pour into a lightly oiled 10x15-inch baking dish, and top with the remaining cheese. Bake at 350 degrees for about 30 minutes or until bubbly.

Note: If you are using fresh herbs, steep them in the 6 cups milk for 10 minutes just as the milk comes to a boil. Then remove and discard the herbs, and proceed with stirring in the grits, butter, and salt.

Makes 18 small servings

In addition to the change in ingredients, I also changed the title of this recipe to Cheddar Cheese, which I do use more often than Gruyère, because while Gruyère is exceptionally better than Cheddar, it is harder to locate in the boondocks, which is where I usually find myself cooking for crowds.

But that's not the real reason I changed the title. The real reason is I wanted it to be the very first recipe in this book, so I can always find it. It is a staple for me. I love it for breakfast and brunches, for barbecues, for grouper and salmon, for a grits boat on my plate with beef stew, and especially all smothered with stewed tomatoes. Frankly, I really need this recipe right here, leading the pack.

Grits and Sausage Casserole

Years ago the Birmingham Chamber of Commerce had me research and write small cookbooklets for their Festival of Arts salute to other countries with whom our city did business. It was amazing how often I came across corn, cornmeal, and variations of what is often thought of as strictly American (and strictly "Southern" in many other places). The names might have been changed to more acceptable-sounding titles, like "polenta" or "stone breads," but essentially ground cornmeal was the reason for the similarities. It is true that, generally speaking, the cornmeal-based breads or dishes were more often found in hot, southern climes like Nigeria, Mexico, and South American countries than, for example, in the colder climates like Germany and Scandinavia. Corn, of course, grows best in southern countries, but with today's global economy, it is usually available almost anywhere in the world.

Maybe it's just the names we give our cornmeal dishes in the southern United States that cause grimaces among our northern diners; after all, "polenta" sounds a lot better than "cornmeal mush," or, to the uninitiated, "grits." To a true Southerner, "grits," "pone," and "corn bread" sound like home. Surely, "greens" and "pot likker" and such can't be far away, even if we ourselves are. In my years of living in New York City, I think I missed grits, corn bread, greens, and sausage the most, especially on Sunday nights when the people we were with ate pizza. Now, years later, you can just about find grits even on very grand occasions at our house, but especially on Sunday.

2 cups water
1 cup milk
2 teaspoons salt
1 cup quick-cooking (not instant) grits
8 ounces shredded sharp Cheddar cheese

1/4 cup (1/2 stick) unsalted butter or low-fat butter substitute
5 eggs, beaten
1 cup milk
1 pound bulk mild or spicy sausage, cooked and drained
4 ounces shredded sharp Cheddar cheese

Bring the water, 1 cup milk, and the salt to a boil in a saucepan. Add the grits in a steady stream, stirring constantly. Cook over medium heat for 5 to 6 minutes, stirring frequently. Let cool slightly; add 8 ounces cheese and the butter and mix well. Stir in 1 cup milk. (This will cool the mixture down enough to add the eggs without cooking them.) Add the eggs, and mix well.

Pour half the mixture into a 3-quart ovenproof casserole. Spread the sausage evenly over the grits in the casserole. Top with the remaining grits. Sprinkle with 4 ounces cheese. Bake at 350 degrees for about 45 minutes or until the top is puffed and golden brown and the mixture is barely pulling away from the sides.

Serves 6 to 8

Grits Soufflé

On her 1960s television programs, Julia Child said, "The point of a soufflé is for the soufflé to collapse before the hostess does." ALL soufflés (and hostesses) do collapse, so time them accordingly. This recipe can be done in small 4- or 6-ounce ramekins, which will cut the cooking time to about 10 minutes. Put the small ramekins on a 10×15-inch baking pan so that they are easier to handle.

2¹/₂ cups milk
2 teaspoons salt
³/₄ cup quick-cooking (not instant) grits
¹/₄ cup unsalted butter
4 egg yolks, beaten
¹/₄ cup grated Parmesan or Romano cheese
6 egg whites
¹/₄ teaspoon cream of tartar

Bring the milk and salt to a boil in a saucepan. Add the grits in a steady stream, stirring constantly. Cook over medium heat for 15 minutes or until the grits are no longer "gritty," stirring frequently. Let cool to the touch. Add the butter and egg yolks, and mix well. Stir in the cheese.

Beat the egg whites with the cream of tartar in a mixer bowl until soft peaks form. Stir about ¹/₂ cup of the egg whites into the grits to lighten the grits; mix gently. Fold in the remaining egg whites, being careful not to deflate the whites.

Pour gently into a lightly oiled straight-sided 1-quart soufflé dish. Bake at 350 degrees for about 35 to 40 minutes or until the soufflé is puffed and barely pulling away from the side of the dish.

Serves 6 to 8

This recipe makes about 6 of the smaller ramekins. This soufflé can also be baked in hollowed-out tomatoes or cooked hollowed-out artichokes. Remember that anything "extra" that goes into a soufflé, like shrimp, crab meat, or small pieces of chicken, must be cooked first. Also, using any more cheese or any particularly fatty foods, such as salmon or bacon, will hold the soufflé down from a very high rise. It will taste fine, but fat keeps the egg whites from rising to great heights. There's more of this soufflé talk in Chapter 3, the Grand Marnier Soufflé (page 148) in particular.

Individual Grits Ramekins

For true Southerners, there are no leftover grits; rather, there are many primary reasons to use cold grits, which are really quite good. One of the best is to cut the cold grits into shapes, just like the Italians cut polenta, and brown the slices in a little olive oil to serve with breakfast or brunch. It is a good change from hash brown potatoes. However, grits are very, very inexpensive, and it is often easier to begin anew for the following ramekins, because, even in the restaurant business, it is almost impossible to have exactly the right amount of leftovers on hand. Let the grits cool before adding the egg whites, or you will end up cooking the egg whites. Remember, too, that grits are terribly bland, and you will need to taste for and add more seasonings than you would with rice or potatoes or pasta. This recipe can be halved.

8 cups chicken broth
1 tablespoon salt
4 garlic cloves, chopped (optional)
1 tablespoon olive oil, Tuscan or
   French if possible
2 teaspoons dry mustard
2 cups quick-cooking (not instant)
   grits

4 large egg yolks
2 cups shredded sharp Cheddar
   cheese (optional)
4 large egg whites
1 teaspoon cream of tartar

Bring the chicken broth, salt, garlic, olive oil and dry mustard to a boil in a saucepan. Add the grits in a steady stream, stirring constantly. Cook until the grits are creamy, stirring frequently. Let cool. Add the egg yolks one at a time, beating well after each addition. Add the cheese.

Beat the egg whites with the cream of tartar in a mixer bowl until stiff peaks form. Fold 1/3 of this mixture into the grits to lighten the grits mixture; then fold the lightened grits mixture into the rest of the beaten egg whites. Combine carefully so as not to break down the egg whites. Pour or spoon into 12 lightly oiled 4-ounce ramekins. Place the ramekins on a baking sheet. Bake at 350 degrees for about 15 minutes or until puffy and bubbly.

To unmold, let cool slightly. Carefully loosen the side of each ramekin. Place a lightly oiled salad plate or other small plate on top of the ramekin; turn the plate over to release the grits onto the plate. (The oil allows you to move the grits mold around on the plate should you need to place it better.)

Serve with Sautéed Shrimp (page 17) or with chicken or country ham.

Serves 12

Sautéed Shrimp for Grits Ramekins

If your family is like ours, with allergies to shrimp or other shellfish, you can substitute smoked salmon for the shrimp and/or very small pieces of smoked or cured ham. I have found that Gwaltney's Virginia hams are sold in thin slices in small packages of 12 or 16 ounces. The smaller packages are very convenient, because with these very salty hams, a little goes a long way. The slices are cured and fully cooked and need only to be frizzled a bit in a skillet to crisp them up. You could use the pieces of crisped ham even if you don't have allergies.

3 tablespoons unsalted butter
3 tablespoons olive oil
4 to 6 green onions, chopped, with some of the green included
1 large garlic clove, smashed
1 pound medium shrimp (size 21-25 if possible), peeled and deveined; or 1 pound boned chicken breasts, lightly pounded and cut into strips
2 cups dry white wine or dry white vermouth

2 tablespoons unsalted butter
Juice of 1 small lemon (about 1 tablespoon)
Salt and pepper to taste
6 to 8 ounces cooked Virginia ham, frizzled as described above (optional); or 6 to 8 ounces good-quality bacon, cooked, drained, and crumbled
5 or 6 sprigs of parsley, rinsed, dried, and finely chopped, for garnish

Heat 3 tablespoons butter and the olive oil in a skillet until hot. Add the green onions, garlic, shrimp, and/or chicken. Cook until the shrimp is firm. Remove the shrimp and chicken, and set aside.

Let the butter and olive oil in the skillet cool slightly. Add the white wine. Cook over high heat until reduced by half. Add 2 tablespoons butter, and the lemon juice, salt, and pepper.

Return the cooked shrimp and chicken to the skillet, and mix well. Pour around the unmolded Individual Grits Ramekins (page 16). Top with the ham, and garnish with the parsley.

Serves 12

Eggs in Red Wine Sauce
(Oeufs en Meurette)

5 slices best-quality bacon
2 onions, chopped
2 cups chopped mushrooms
2 garlic cloves, chopped
1 bay leaf
1 teaspoon dried thyme, or 1 tablespoon fresh thyme
3 cups good red wine
2 (10-ounce) cans beef consommé
2 teaspoons sugar
Salt and pepper to taste
8 slices good-quality white bread, toasted, crusts removed, and
   cut into triangles
½ cup (1 stick) unsalted butter, melted
2 tablespoons (or more) good-quality olive oil
6 eggs

Fry the bacon in a skillet; remove from the skillet, and drain well. Crumble into fairly large pieces, and set aside.

Cook the onions, mushrooms, and garlic in the skillet until wilted. Add the bay leaf, thyme, wine, consommé, and sugar. Cook over high heat until the liquid is reduced by about half. Taste for seasoning before adding any salt and pepper; it may already be quite salty from the bacon.

Line a 9x13-inch ovenproof casserole with the toast triangles. Pour the melted butter and 2 tablespoons olive oil over the toast. Pour the wine sauce evenly over the toast, spreading evenly.

Break the eggs into the sauce in the casserole, making 2 rows of 3. If the sauce does not cover each egg, pour 1 teaspoon additional olive oil over each egg yolk. (This will keep them from drying out during baking.)

Bake at 350 degrees for 20 to 30 minutes or until all the eggs are set. Sprinkle the crumbled bacon evenly over the top before serving.

Serves 4 to 6

"A meurette is a pungent red wine sauce, which originated in Burgundy. It is well seasoned with bacon and garlic. Eggs are poached in this sauce and served on fine 'croutons' of bread fried in butter. This dish makes an excellent appetizer for an elegant dinner or makes a glamorous lunch. Maybe it tastes best of all served at the beginning of an intimate little candlelit supper for two." M. Guidroz, **Adventures in French Cooking**, *page 53.*

*M*yriam Guidroz was my first and favorite cooking teacher. She taught cooking in her New Orleans home in the early 1960s, when I was a new bride and literally could not make a pot of coffee. Her easy, practical, economical style of teaching was just what I needed, and, of course, all the indigenous products of New Orleans were a great help to a non-cook, too.

Ms. Guidroz and her family had fled the Nazi invasion of their Belgian homeland in the 1940s. She and her family lived in England until the end of World War II, and ultimately they relocated in New Orleans. Because of the War, her family had had to get by on very little; therefore, Ms. Guidroz became a very wise and frugal cook.

She was exactly the kind of teacher I needed when I was learning to cook for my own family. My husband was in medical school at Tulane, and we were very poor. Ms. Guidroz's classes were one of the best investments I've ever made. I mentioned her often in my first book, Remembrances of Things Passed. When the book was published, I sent her one of the first copies. She graciously called me upon receiving it. It was a real blessing for me to thank her personally for all my treasured remembrances of her. Only a few weeks later, Ms. Guidroz died. She had been terminally ill for several years. Now it is like St. Paul said, I "thank my God upon my every remembrance of" her.

This is her recipe, which I have necessarily adapted somewhat. Even so, mine will never taste as good as hers. Do like she did, and serve it on homemade croutons, "fried toast," as she called it.

Bakery Scrambled Eggs

Because we always said, "There are no mistakes in a bakery, just more crumbs," we of course hit upon this recipe/technique/whatever by all-natural causes. During the years of my restaurant, take-out shop, bakery, catering business, et al. (all in one business, of course), we also had High Tea on Tuesday afternoons. "High Tea" is not like "High Church" or "high fashion"; rather, it is typically an early evening family-type meal and almost always includes ham, an egg dish, and a sweet of some sort.

In those days, we had seemingly tons of croissant crumbs all the time. We breaded fish, chicken, vegetables, crab cakes, and the floor with them those eight years or so. Croissant crumbs were especially good, oddly enough, in scrambled eggs for High Tea.

Serve this big omelet with neatly chopped Roma tomatoes or the Tomato Salsa on page 22 if you prefer a savory omelet. My family's favorite addition is to spread our slices with Cheddar cheese and guava jelly.

6 eggs, or an equivalent amount of egg substitute
2 cups whole milk or skim milk
2 teaspoons Tabasco sauce (optional)
40 saltines, crushed
Salt and pepper to taste
1/4 cup olive oil, vegetable oil, or butter

Beat the eggs, milk, and Tabasco sauce in a bowl. Add the saltine crumbs. Let stand for about 10 minutes. Season with salt and pepper. Remember to allow for the salt in the crackers.

Heat the olive oil in a large nonstick skillet. Add the egg mixture. Cook over medium heat until the eggs are set, stirring gently. Loosen the edges. If possible, turn the omelet over in one big turn. If not, cut it into 2 large pieces and flip each piece individually. Both sides should be slightly browned.

Serve in pie-shaped wedges.

Serves 8

Years after my restaurant days, as a bed-and-breakfast chef in a remote northwest Alabama town, I had no hope of fresh croissant crumbs, but we had an over-abundance of saltine crackers. Actually, I think the saltines were better than the croissant crumbs, and the saltines were certainly lower in fat. For our health-conscious guests, I used egg substitute and really seasoned the whole thing with fresh herbs from our Sand Mountain garden. Chopped basil, dill, cilantro, thyme, and a pinch or two of dry mustard make a wonderful low-fat breakfast dish. Some saltines are lower in fat and salt than others, should you want to reduce those two ingredients even more.

Cottage Cheese Baked Eggs

Chloe, one of our grandchildren, has always loved cottage cheese, even as an infant. We fix these eggs for her and for ourselves, because they are very high in protein and calcium. If you are on a fat-free diet, egg substitute and low-fat cottage cheese are just as good as the real thing.

Evans, Chloe's dad and our youngest son, always stood up for his grownup tastes as a child, too. While they were growing up, Evans' two older brothers, Charles and John, could not make Evans give up his taste for cabbage, brussels sprouts, eggplant, and all manner of grownup foods, no matter how hard they tried. Who do you think is the best chef of the three today? Evans has even had wonderful press for his expertise, too. JoEllen O'Hara of The Birmingham News *did a wonderful cover story in the food section about Evans and his gourmet-ness. With her confidence and sense of adventure, even if Chloe does not become a chef, she sure should be a good cook like her dad.*

8 eggs, beaten
1 cup cottage cheese, drained
2 tablespoons chopped fresh chives
2 teaspoons dill
Salt and freshly ground pepper to taste
4 slices homemade bread, toasted on both sides
3 tablespoons unsalted butter, melted

Combine the eggs, cottage cheese, chives, dill, salt, and pepper in a bowl, and mix well. Line a small ovenproof dish with the toasted bread. Pour the melted butter evenly over the toast. Pour the cottage cheese mixture over the toast. Bake at 350 degrees for 20 minutes or until the eggs are set and a knife inserted near the center comes out clean.

Serves 4 to 6

These eggs can be scrambled in a large skillet with the cottage cheese mixed in. Of course, scrambling takes a lot less time, but it must be done at the last minute. If you are not rushed in the morning, by all means scramble the eggs. It seems early morning breakfasts or brunches need a lot of last-minute attention from me, so I prefer to run the eggs in the oven while I down a cup or two of coffee.

Eggs and Tomato Salsa

If your menu for breakfast or brunch is a little heavy on the bread side, you may want to make this salsa ahead, and then simply scramble the eggs just before serving, rather than baking them over the toast as in this recipe. If everything else is done, plain scrambled eggs take only a few minutes. When I am cooking for more than ten people, I usually scramble two batches of eggs, so that the eggs won't get cold.

However I prepare the eggs, plain scrambled or, as here, baked on toast, I serve the salsa in a pretty glass pedestal bowl, which I place on the buffet in between the cheese grits and the eggs. You don't want to confuse people too early in the morning, and if you put the salsa by a bowl of fresh fruit, for example, some sleepyhead just may put it on the fruit and think you've got strange tastes indeed. This recipe serves about ten people, and you can divide it exactly in half if you so desire. Rather than doubling it for more people, I would make two casseroles. They bake better and keep warmer if they are not larger than 10x13 inches.

8 slices whole grain bread, toasted
1/2 cup good-quality olive oil
1 cup any one or any combination
   of grated Romano, Parmesan,
   or asiago cheese

1 tablespoon salt
1 tablespoon cracked pepper
10 large eggs, beaten
Tomato Salsa (below)

Line a 10x13-inch baking dish with the toast, trimmed to fit if needed. Sprinkle with the olive oil and half the cheese. Stir the salt and pepper into the eggs, and pour over the toast. Top with the remaining cheese. Bake at 350 degrees for 25 to 30 minutes or until the eggs are set. Serve with Tomato Salsa on the side.

Serves 8 to 10

Tomato Salsa

1 large sweet onion, chopped
2 large ribs celery, peeled and
   chopped
1 large garlic clove, chopped
1/4 cup olive oil

2 cups chopped, seeded, and
   peeled tomatoes
1 bunch fresh cilantro, coarsely
   chopped
Salt and pepper to taste

Sauté the onion, celery, and garlic in the olive oil in a skillet until the vegetables begin to wilt somewhat. Add the tomatoes. Cook over high heat for 3 to 5 minutes to reduce the liquid. Add the cilantro, salt, and pepper. Serve hot or at room temperature. This is also excellent on Cheddar Cheese Grits (page 13).

Makes about 2 cups

Ham and Broccoli Frittata

1/2 cup (1 stick) unsalted butter, melted
10 slices very thin white bread, crusts removed
   (preferably brioche or other homemade bread)
2 cups shredded Cheddar cheese
2 cups cooked chopped broccoli
10 eggs, beaten
1 tablespoon Dijon mustard
1 tablespoon salt
Freshly ground pepper to taste
1 teaspoon Tabasco sauce
1 tablespoon Worcestershire sauce
3 cups milk

Butter each slice of bread on 1 side, and cut the bread into cubes.
Place in a large ovenproof casserole. Cover the bread with the cheese.
Top with the broccoli.

Combine the eggs, Dijon mustard, salt, pepper, Tabasco sauce,
Worcestershire sauce, and milk in a bowl, and mix well. Pour over
the ingredients in the casserole, adding more milk if needed to cover
all the bread. Chill in the refrigerator for 8 hours to overnight.

Bake at 375 degrees for 40 to 45 minutes or until the top is puffed and
golden brown and a knife inserted near the center comes out clean.
If the frittata begins to darken, cover loosely with foil to prevent
overbrowning.

The frittata can be held for 15 to 20 minutes, but it will lose its puffiness.

Serves 6 to 8

Potato and Onion Frittata

Every country has its own version of a large "potato cake," with or without eggs baked in it. In Spain, it is often called a tortilla, though vastly different from our American Tex-Mex idea of the flour- or cornmeal-based bread of the same name. In the South of the United States, it is often simply called a "bake." "Frittata," which is Italian, is fairly universally used to describe the following dish, which does include eggs. Call it what you will, it is a real comfort food and a great company dish, too. I have here called for precooking the potatoes to make it a do-ahead dish. Precooking the potatoes also keeps them from turning dark.

2 pounds Yukon gold or red potatoes
1/4 cup olive oil
1 large Vidalia onion or other sweet onion, thinly sliced
3 or 4 garlic cloves, chopped, or 1 elephant garlic clove, chopped
2 teaspoons dill
Salt and freshly ground pepper to taste
8 large eggs, beaten
1/2 cup grated Parmesan or Romano cheese, or a combination of the two

Boil the unpeeled potatoes in water to cover in a saucepan for about 30 minutes or until a knife can barely pierce through each potato. Do not overcook. Drain well, and let cool. Peel and thoroughly dry the potatoes.

Slice the potatoes no thicker than 1/4 inch, and place them in a lightly oiled ovenproof casserole.

Heat the olive oil in a skillet. Add the onion slices and garlic. Cook over low heat until the onion is translucent and the garlic is wilted but not browned.

Spoon the onion slices, garlic, and olive oil over the potatoes. Beat the dill, salt, and pepper into the eggs. Pour over the potatoes, and mix gently.

Bake at 350 degrees for 35 to 40 minutes or until the eggs are set. Top with the cheese.

Serves 4 to 6

Bacon that has been cooked, drained, and crumbled can be sprinkled over the finished frittata. This frittata cooks best in a fairly shallow ovenproof casserole. The one I use is round, and even though the frittata is served in its dish, it has more of the authentic Spanish "tortilla" shape than a rectangular dish. Often the Spanish tortilla is served unmolded and sliced like a pie. It is a little easier to manage leaving it in the casserole as I do here. Tomato Salsa (page 22) is wonderful with this. I have seen a few six-year-olds put ketchup on it, but you don't have to noise that abroad.

Sausage and Cheese Frittata

Kris, our daughter-in-law, entertains a lot more than I do these days. I am always asking her for what's new, good, and easy. This is one of her Christmas favorites, because it should be done the night before. In the summers when we are all at the beach, she serves it for us on Sundays, when we have our one big brunch, and we love it. There are quite a few types of sausage that can be used that are not too spicy. Some are even low-fat, like some of the turkey sausages, but we think holidays might have some kind of dispensation from calories and such. It's a happy thought, anyway.

8 slices white bread, crusts removed and cut into cubes
1 pound sausage, cooked, drained, and crumbled
10 large eggs
2 cups milk
1 tablespoon Worcestershire sauce
2 teaspoons (scant) Tabasco sauce
2 teaspoons salt
Freshly ground pepper to taste
2 cups shredded Cheddar cheese

Lightly oil a 10x13-inch baking dish. Place the bread cubes in the dish. Spread the sausage evenly over the bread.

Mix the eggs, milk, Worcestershire sauce, Tabasco sauce, salt, and pepper in a bowl. Pour over the bread, pushing down any pieces that float in order to soak all the bread cubes. Spread the cheese over the top. Chill for 2 hours or longer, or overnight if possible.

Bake at 350 degrees for about 45 to 60 minutes or until puffed and golden brown. Let stand for 10 minutes before serving. It will deflate somewhat, but the cheese will cool off enough to eat.

Serves 6 to 8

Green or black olives, 1 cup of very well-drained tomatoes, or cooked and drained asparagus adds a lot of flavor to this dish. It needs something spicy with a good texture. I have found that, even with this many eggs, sautéed fresh mushrooms tend to be too watery to hold together well. I have eaten it with homemade chili with black olives and Mexican cheese, and that was wonderful, too. Serve it then with an avocado salad.

Poaching Eggs

Obviously, poaching and scrambling eggs are stove-top methods rather than baking, as this book implies. These stove-top egg dishes can be served with or actually ON some of the true baking recipes, such as the hashes, biscuits, and pancakes. I just could not leave out these basic egg-cooking recipes. In New Orleans, we would call these and other nonconforming recipes "lagniappe," that is, something extra, a bonus.

In my first book, Remembrances of Things Passed, *I discussed how to poach and hold eggs overnight. All my years in New Orleans taught me that the only way to serve poached eggs is to keep a bowl of ice water nearby and put the finished poached egg in the ice water. You can trim them up nicely with a pair of scissors once they are cold. Putting the eggs in warm water reheats them easily. Be sure to dry them off gently with a clean towel before putting them on the plate. When you have a lot to do very early in the morning, poaching eggs can be very irksome. They never seem to cooperate nicely in the early mornings: They break easily, look unsightly, or do something else for which you really don't have the time. Doing them the night before is a lot easier on the nerves.*

So, have the water just barely simmering, add 1 tablespoon of white vinegar and 1 teaspoon of salt, then gently slide the raw egg into the water. My largest skillet will take about 6 eggs at one time. Using a large spoon, baste the yolks gently with the simmering water to cook the tops of the yolks. When the eggs are cooked to your liking, remove each one gently from the simmering water with a slotted spoon and slide the egg into the big bowl of ice water. Trim with scissors if desired. Replenish the ice as necessary to keep the eggs cold. Refrigerate until needed.

Poached eggs are great with corned beef hash or on little triangles of fried bread or Holland rusks for all the New Orleans-type egg dishes, such as Eggs Benedict and Eggs Hussarde. My personal favorite is Eggs Sardou.

For Eggs Sardou, line a cooked artichoke bottom with cooked creamed spinach, top with a poached egg, and top the whole thing with Hollandaise sauce or a warmed homemade lemon mayonnaise.

Cold poached eggs in a homemade aspic in ramekins are classic French Oeufs en Gelée and are still comfort food for me.

Red Flannel Hash

"Why red flannel?" is always the question about this wonderful dish, and, as usual, I have an idea why it is thusly named. The "red," of course, comes from the grated beets, and since some men have a fierce aversion to beets (for no really good reason), some pioneer woman wised up and said, "It's red flannel hash, good for getting out of your red flannel pajamas every morning." Yeah, right. Anyhow, it is not a beet dish; it's a hash dish, and it's delicious. If you, the cook, are a beet person and your recipients aren't, try this hash first (and don't tell them until later).

Then, by all means, bake the real Red Velvet Cake in Chapter 3 of this book (page 102). Originally, it was "red velvet" cake because it was made with beets (like carrots in a carrot cake) and never, ever because of a whole bottle of red food coloring. As my sister in Nashville notes on quite a few of her recipe asides: "Yuck. Nasty. Where did this come from? Who knows?" And that's the truth about red food coloring in Red Velvet Cake, but I'm not swearing to you about the red flannel hash thing. It's beets, though, and I will swear to that.

4 medium red beets, cooked, then cubed or shredded
3 medium golden potatoes, cooked, then cubed or shredded
2 pounds cooked corned beef, cut into bite-size cubes
2 eggs, beaten
1/2 cup heavy cream
2 teaspoons Tabasco sauce
1 tablespoon Worcestershire sauce
Salt and freshly ground pepper to taste
3 tablespoons olive oil or vegetable oil
1 medium Vidalia onion or other sweet onion, chopped
2 garlic cloves, minced
3 ribs celery, chopped
1/2 cup heavy cream

Mix the beets, potatoes, and corned beef in a bowl. Add the eggs, 1/2 cup cream, the Tabasco sauce, Worcestershire sauce, salt, and pepper, and mix as you would for meat loaf.

Heat the olive oil in a skillet. Add the onion, garlic, and celery, and sauté until they are limp but still have some texture. Let cool slightly. Add to the corned beef mixture, and mix well.

Pack the hash into a 9-inch glass pie plate or square baking pan. The hash should be about 2 to 3 inches thick. Pour 1/2 cup cream over the top. Let stand for a few minutes to allow the cream to seep into the hash.

Bake at 350 degrees for about 35 minutes for a pie plate or about 40 minutes for a deeper pan.

Serves 4 to 6

This hash is quite good served with poached eggs (see page 26 for directions on poaching eggs ahead of time). Or, you can bake the eggs into the hash after 15 minutes of baking. Simply press holes in the hash with the back of a large serving spoon, and break the eggs carefully into the hash. Drizzle a small amount of the cream over the top of each egg. Bake for about 20 minutes longer or until the eggs are done. Serve with Tomato Salsa (page 22) or, as our family prefers, with plain ketchup.

Corned Beef Hash

Right after St. Patrick's Day, when we have had our annual corned beef and cabbage, we get the added bonus of corned beef hash for Sunday night supper or, of course, for brunch. Any other time of the year, a good deli brand of cooked corned beef works well. Ask the deli not to slice it as thin as for sandwiches, but leave it in a two-pound piece so that you can get the requisite hashed corned beef. You can chop it into thick chunks or really hash it up with a sharp chef's knife. We like small chunks best.

3 tablespoons corn oil or other vegetable oil
1 large onion, chopped (about 1 cup)
2 tablespoons chopped fresh garlic
3 ribs celery, chopped (about 1/2 cup)
1/2 cup chopped parsley
1 tablespoon dried thyme, or 2 tablespoons chopped fresh thyme

1 cup peeled and chopped tomatoes
2 pounds cooked corned beef, cut into chunks or hashed
1 pound potatoes, peeled, diced, and cooked (about 3 cups)
Salt and pepper to taste
2 large eggs, beaten
1/2 cup toasted plain bread crumbs
Corn oil

Heat 3 tablespoons corn oil in a skillet. Add the onion, garlic, and celery, and sauté just until tender. Add the parsley, thyme, and tomatoes. Cook over medium heat until the liquid is somewhat reduced. Add the corned beef and potatoes, and mix well. Season with salt and pepper.

Let stand until the mixture is cool enough not to cook the eggs. Add the eggs and bread crumbs, and mix well. Shape into patties. Refrigerate until serving time.

Heat a small amount of corn oil in a skillet. Add the patties, and cook until the patties are browned on both sides and the beef is heated through.

Serve with Tomato Salsa (page 22) and poached, scrambled, or fried eggs.

Makes 8 to 10 patties

Oatmeal Soufflé

Oatmeal was always my childhood food of choice, my absolute comfort food, and now the American Heart Association freely encourages oatmeal even for the calorie-conscious among us. This recipe for Oatmeal Soufflé is admittedly a lighter version of my original comfort-oatmeal, with its butter, cream, and brown sugar, but it is good enough to persuade some pretty serious doubters. I find it very popular with the heart-healthy people, and not just because of its newly declared benefits. If you want to use steel-cut oats, follow the directions on the package for the initial cooking, because they take a lot longer to cook than other oats.

2 cups skim milk or whole milk
1/4 cup unsalted butter or butter substitute
1 1/2 cups quick-cooking (not instant) oats
8 ounces Neufchâtel, low-fat, or nonfat cream cheese, softened
1 teaspoon salt
1 cup good-quality pure maple syrup
1 teaspoon cinnamon
1 teaspoon nutmeg
1 tablespoon vanilla extract
1 cup egg substitute, or 4 egg yolks
1/4 cup egg white powder, rehydrated with 1 cup water, or 4 egg whites
1 teaspoon cream of tartar
1 cup toasted chopped pecans (optional)

Bring the milk to a boil in a saucepan. Stir in the butter and oats. Cook until thick, stirring constantly. Add the cream cheese, salt, maple syrup, cinnamon, nutmeg, and vanilla, and mix well. Let cool slightly. Stir in the egg substitute.

Beat the egg whites with the cream of tartar in a mixer bowl until soft peaks form. Fold the egg whites into the oatmeal. Spoon the oatmeal into a lightly oiled 2-quart soufflé dish. Top with the toasted pecans; cover the pecans lightly with some of the oatmeal so that they do not burn during baking.

Bake at 350 degrees for about 40 minutes or until a knife inserted near the center comes out clean.

Serves 8 to 10

Long, long ago, seemingly now in a galaxy far away, I can remember being admonished by our pediatrician to gain weight. I can hardly imagine that today. Of course, that was before the last two years of high school, when it became exceptionally easy to comply with Dr. Simpson's advice. It seems that in my later teens, I was eating less and gaining more, and all my old favorites were outlawed by the calorie police. I'm so glad oatmeal is back in favor.

Oatmeal Granola

This granola keeps well if you let it cool down and keep it in large-mouth Mason jars, in either the refrigerator or freezer. It is wonderful for desserts like brown Betty or rice pudding or mixed in with flavored yogurt or as a topping for yogurt. I especially like it on baked fruits, like apples, pears, fresh cherries, peaches, strawberries, and rhubarb, that, once cooked, lose their texture.

Granola's sweetness, and especially its texture, adds a lot of satisfaction to otherwise plain foods. Texture or chewiness adds a great deal to the satiety rate of food, which simply means that you enjoy feeling satisfied more quickly than with foods without much texture. Of course, smoothness in texture (like ice cream and custards) has its place, but things that are smooth and go down real easy (like milkshakes and poured custards) can be very, very caloric.

➤

2 pounds rolled oats (about 10 cups)
2 cups (1 pound) oat flakes, large flakes if possible
2 cups raw sunflower seeds, hulled
2 cups sliced almonds
2 cups chopped pecans, walnuts, or plain peanuts (optional)
1 cup shredded coconut, sweetened to taste
1 cup golden raisins, dried cranberries, or dried cherries
1 cup safflower oil, or any other plain unsaturated oil
2 cups honey
1 cup dark molasses (not blackstrap)
1 tablespoon vanilla extract
2 teaspoons cinnamon
2 teaspoons cardamom
2 teaspoons nutmeg
2 teaspoons crystallized ginger (optional)
Salt to taste

Combine the oats, oat flakes, sunflower seeds, almonds, pecans, coconut, and raisins in a large bowl, and mix well.

Heat the safflower oil, honey, molasses, vanilla, cinnamon, cardamom, nutmeg, and crystallized ginger in a saucepan, stirring to mix well. Pour over the oat mixture, and mix well. Taste for seasonings, especially salt.

Spread the granola in a lightly oiled foil-lined 10x15-inch baking pan. Bake at 275 degrees for about 1 hour, stirring with a flat spatula at regular intervals. Remove from the oven when slightly toasted but not dark. Do not let the ingredients darken or harden.

Store in a wide-mouthed Mason jar, or, if you will be using the granola within a week, store in zip-top plastic bags. Seal the plastic bags as airtight as possible to keep the granola from hardening. If it does harden, add a cup or so of raisins or other dried fruit to rehydrate the granola somewhat.

Makes about 4 quarts

It is no small matter that I take so well to oatmeal. My mother's maiden name and my middle (maiden) name is OATES. Mother's best friend and roommate at National Cathedral, which was then a college, was Martha Bray (Dobbs), and of course Bray and Oates from the South opened the doors to all sorts of thick Southern accents (and a lot of big lies, too, about their heritage). Who in Washington, D.C., would ever check up on them? Every single one of them, that's who.

My grandmother, Ellie Oates, and Martha's mother, Emma Kate Bray, cooked up a lot of grits, corn bread, turnip greens, and dumplings when Mother and Martha brought all those "Yankee girls" home to Alabama.

My grandmother was about 4'10" and weighed 80 pounds, so my grandfather did have a driver for her long black Cadillac, à la Driving Miss Daisy. Emma Kate was equally impressive when I knew her years later, so I am sure she really played the part, too, for Mother and Martha. This, of course, only added fuel to the girls' wacky fires, while they were away at school during the Depression years.

I bet they never dreamed of granola! It was a derogatory term when I was in college in New Orleans in the 1950s and '60s, because we had a LOT of beatniks/hippies/Goth-types (a lot of us were and some of us still are, as a matter of fact), whom we called The Granolas. Now they are all successful potters and artists of all types. Newcomb Art School is a very famous art school, and it has been for almost a hundred years. It must have been the oatmeal.

(continued)

When I worked as a chef, I often had to cook for people who, because of chemotherapy, oral surgery, or other problems, could only eat or drink smooth foods. In those cases, I puréed stewed cooked fruits; seasoned vegetables to the hilt with mild herbs; and put aside any thoughts of texture. Oatmeal can be quite good, just plain, cooked from the directions on the back of the package, and, if necessary, puréed as well. In that case, season it with brown sugar, butter if they can tolerate it, vanilla, and especially salt.

Vegetable Roulade

This roulade is wonderful with a good green salad with only a few cherry or Roma tomatoes and a good vinaigrette. I like to use ¹/4 cup balsamic vinegar with 1 cup olive oil, about 2 teaspoons salt, and freshly ground pepper to taste.

Toss the salad with the vinaigrette, and be sure it is well seasoned, especially with salt. Do not drown the salad, but be sure each leaf is well coated. Then arrange the green salad around the warm roulade on the serving platter. Serve at once.

The vinaigrette gets all bogged into the roulade, and it is heaven! After all, Frasier sings about "tossed salad and scrambled eggs." A wonderful accompaniment is Nueske's applewood-smoked bacon, which you can put in the oven at the same time as the roulade. Then your hands are free for 15 minutes to set the orange juice and coffee out on the table (or have a cup of coffee for yourself).

➤

8 egg yolks
3 cups sliced vegetables, such as carrots, fresh beets,
   asparagus, English peas, and celery, cooked until no moisture remains
¹/2 cup (1 stick) unsalted butter or butter substitute suitable
   for cooking, melted
1 tablespoon salt
Freshly ground pepper to taste
2 teaspoons Tabasco sauce
¹/4 cup chopped fresh cilantro
¹/4 cup chopped fresh parsley
¹/4 cup chopped chives or tops of green onions
8 egg whites
2 teaspoons salt
¹/8 teaspoon cream of tartar
Cherry tomatoes, for garnish
Fresh herbs such as parsley, rosemary, or cilantro, for garnish

Oil a 12x17-inch baking pan, and line with waxed paper or parchment paper. Lightly oil the paper.

Beat the egg yolks in a mixer bowl until thick and pale yellow. Add the cooked vegetables, melted butter, 1 tablespoon salt, the pepper, Tabasco sauce, cilantro, parsley, and chives, and mix well.

Beat the egg whites, 2 teaspoons salt, and the cream of tartar in a mixer bowl until the whites mound up but are not separating. Lighten the egg yolk mixture with about 1 cup of the beaten egg whites; then fold the egg whites into the egg yolk mixture.

Pour gently into the baking pan, being sure to fill in all 4 corners so they won't burn. Bake at 350 degrees for 15 to 18 minutes or until the center springs back when lightly touched. Remove from the oven, and let cool very slightly. Lightly oil a serving platter so that you can move the roulade around on the platter if necessary.

Start from the longer side and roll into a neat tube, using the paper on the baking pan as your guide. Make the final turn of the roll onto the prepared platter. Reposition carefully if needed. Garnish with cherry tomatoes and fresh herbs.

Serves 4 to 6

Virginia, a.k.a. Gigi, my sister in Nashville, sent me this recipe, which I had forgotten all about. That's a good sister.

This roulade is a lot simpler than the Mushroom Roulade on page 34. Here, it is all rolled into one roulade with no filling, but it could have just a sauce over the top. The Tomato Salsa on page 22 is delicious with the eggs and vegetables.

It is important to get as much liquid as possible out of the cooked vegetables that are stirred into the egg mixture, or the roulade won't work. Before I ran a restaurant, I used to squeeze the vegetables out in a clean dish towel, but I found that high heat in a heavy skillet or sauté pan will get all the liquid out quicker and more thoroughly than a dish towel. Be very careful, however, not to scorch the vegetables. Stir them the whole time, because it doesn't take very long to scorch them.

You can use any vegetables in any proportions that you and yours like best. Chopped red, yellow, and orange peppers sautéed in olive oil and seasoned with herbs would be "Pipérade." Spinach sautéed and seasoned would be "Florentine." Spring vegetables, such as cooked English peas and cooked shredded baby carrots, would be "Printemps," or "Springtime."

My three cups of vegetables here are just suggestions. They must be cooked, and they must be dried of all cooking liquid. Meats work well, too—chopped cooked smoked turkey, ham, even very small shrimp—as do bite-size cheeses. Eggs and egg whites are very bland, so season them highly. Keep in mind that fresh herbs like basil are very watery. I have used cilantro, parsley, and chives, because they do not have a lot of moisture in them. Dried herbs are fine, but garnish with the chopped fresh ones if you have them.

(continued)

Nueske's bacon (see page 171 under Sources) is exceptional. I put it in another baking pan lined with foil and bake it at 350 degrees for 45 minutes. About 2/3 of the way through the cooking time, I put dark brown sugar over each piece to caramelize the brown sugar without burning it. Until it cools, be very careful moving it and also keep all would-be tasters away from it: Hot bacon and hot sugar are lethal. (I don't know why we all feel free to help ourselves to any bacon that is cooked and within our reach. Everyone does, though, so prepare a lot.)

The combination of sweet and salty bacon, crisp vinegary salad, and smooth eggs with crunchy vegetables is a real success. A really good sweet roll, or Pecan Cinnamon Roll (page 83), with sweet unsalted butter makes the day! Bless and eat!

Mushroom Roulade

3 tablespoons olive oil or
   vegetable oil
4 green onions, chopped, with
   some of the green included
3 ribs celery, chopped
1 garlic clove, chopped
2 cups chopped fresh mushrooms
2 teaspoons thyme
2 teaspoons tarragon
Salt and freshly ground pepper to
   taste
3 tablespoons unsalted butter
3 tablespoons all-purpose flour
1 1/2 cups milk

1/2 cup heavy cream
Dash of Tabasco sauce
2 teaspoons freshly ground
   nutmeg
6 egg yolks
1 cup any one or any combination
   of grated Romano, Parmesan,
   or asiago cheese, or other hard
   white cheese
Salt and freshly ground pepper
   to taste
6 egg whites
1/2 cup grated hard white cheese
Chopped fresh parsley, for garnish

For the mushroom filling, heat the olive oil in a large skillet. Add the green onions, celery, garlic, mushrooms, thyme, and tarragon to the skillet. Cook until the vegetables are wilted and the mushroom liquid has evaporated. Season with salt and pepper. Set aside, and let cool.

For the roulade, lightly oil a 10x15-inch baking pan. Line the pan with oiled waxed paper or parchment paper. Melt the butter in a skillet. Add the flour all at once. Cook until the flour is cooked but not at all browned, stirring frequently. Add the milk and cream, whisking until smooth. Cook for several minutes or until any taste or smell of the flour is gone and the mixture is beginning to thicken. Add the Tabasco sauce and nutmeg. Remove from the heat. Let stand until cool to the touch.

Whisk the egg yolks into the cooled flour mixture. Add 1 cup cheese. Season with salt and pepper. This is a bland mixture and needs quite a bit of seasoning.

Beat the egg whites in a large mixer bowl until soft peaks form. Gently stir in 1/3 of the cheese mixture at a time, being careful not to deflate the egg whites. Spoon into the prepared pan. Bake at 350 degrees for about 15 minutes or until the roulade is puffed and pulling away from the edges.

Let the roulade cool slightly. Use the waxed paper to move the roulade onto an ovenproof platter. Spread the mushroom filling evenly over the roulade. Use the waxed paper to roll lengthwise into a long tube with the seam on the bottom. Remove and discard the waxed paper.

Top with 1/2 cup cheese. Reheat, covered loosely, at 325 degrees for 10 minutes. Be careful not to dry out the roulade. Garnish with the parsley.

Serves 4 to 6

This roulade is wonderful with a tomato sauce and/or additional sautéed fresh mushrooms. In France, it is not unusual to serve it cold or at room temperature. It must be highly flavored, however, to serve it cold, as eggs tend to be quite bland if not seasoned well. Whether it is served hot or cold, any of these are great companions to this roulade: grilled sweet red or yellow peppers in a good olive oil; olives in a tapenade; even cooked seasoned shrimp. It can be a wonderful first course at dinner or a side dish with chicken or fish dishes. Obviously, it is quite versatile, and because it can be prepared ahead and reheated, it is a real time-saver, too.

Julie Dannenbaum was one of my favorite cooking teachers. Julie taught for several years at the fabulous Greenbriar in West Virginia, but she had my idea of an ideal cooking school on Walnut Street in Philadelphia. My sister, Virginia, and I attended many of Julie's classes at both places, and we still use and appreciate many of the things we learned from her.

Julie's Northern Italian classes were instrumental in moving me away from my Francophile years to becoming a true and long-lasting Italophile. Northern Italian was not very popular in American cooking classes in the early 1970s, but thanks to the likes of Julie, the Greenbriar, and others who sang the Italian siren song, Milanese, Sienese, and Tuscan have become household favorites in America, too.

"Roulade," of course, is as French as it can be, but Julie was the spokesperson for Campbell's soups at the time, and she made this rolled soufflé from one of the Campbell soup products. Over the years, the recipe evolved into what I have here: sort of an eclectic dish. How American can you get?! This is wonderful served with a green salad and fresh fruit.

Breakfast Tortillas

Many years ago, when I was in the restaurant business, we also ran a cooking school three times a year. Occasionally, large organizations like the Junior League or the Service Guild would have very important chefs and celebrities come to Birmingham to give a very large demonstration series. Our staff was usually called to be the prep and assistant team for the visiting dignitaries, which was time-consuming but a lot of fun. One particular VIP canceled his demonstration at the very last minute, and some of the Brennan family in New Orleans put together a wonderful last-minute team of four, the Brennans included, to appease and satisfy the crowds. And did they ever!

One of the fabulous "emergency team" was Anne Lindsay Greer from Texas, a food writer and media personality, who had written a wonderful book entitled Cuisine of the American Southwest. *Besides being such a lovely person, Anne also brought a wonderful repertoire of ideas, tastes, and good ol' fresh air to a very "Frenchified" era in the Food Revolution. I think the Brennans and Anne knew they were pacesetters even back then, but I wonder if they ever dreamed the Latino influence would be so wonderfully present as it is in this new millennium. This breakfast casserole is a very loose translation of Anne's original ideas so many years ago, but as with everything, that's the point.*

6 large tortilla "bowls" (see Note)	1 1/2 cups milk
2 tablespoons vegetable oil	2 tablespoons tomato paste
1 large Vidalia onion, chopped	2 teaspoons salt
2 ribs celery, chopped	2 teaspoons freshly ground pepper
1 1/2 cups peeled and coarsely chopped tomatoes	2 cups shredded Monterey Jack cheese
1 cup mild or hot green chiles, seeded (drain if using canned)	3 cups shredded Cheddar cheese
6 eggs, beaten	1 bunch cilantro, chopped, for garnish

Place the tortilla bowls on a heavy baking sheet. Place in a 300-degree oven while you prepare the filling. Heat the vegetable oil in a large skillet. Add the onion and celery, and sauté just until wilted. Add the tomatoes and chiles. Cook over medium heat until most of the liquid is reduced. Let cool slightly. Add the eggs, milk, tomato paste, salt, pepper, Monterey Jack cheese, and 2 cups of the Cheddar cheese, and mix well. Spoon into the tortilla bowls. Increase the oven temperature to 375 degrees. Return the filled tortilla bowls to the oven. Bake for 35 to 40 minutes or until the filling in each bowl is set. Top with the remaining 1 cup Cheddar cheese. Garnish with the chopped cilantro. Serve within 1 hour.

Note: Tortilla "bowls" are usually found in the dairy case of the supermarket.

Serves 6

Chicken Curry with Raita

This is the traditional chicken curry that is generally served over white or yellow rice. It is very popular for brunches or Sunday night suppers, even among the self-avowed curry haters. I have a lot of alternatives in the menu for the "haters," but I have not seen too many guests avoid the curries I serve. I do have all the fussy accompaniments, like mango chutney, chopped green onions, even the Italian mostarda di frutta (mustard fruit), raisins, and chopped bananas sprinkled with lemon juice. You can add peanuts, coconut, and chopped apples, for even more little bowls around the curry and the rice.

Therefore, if there are those who don't like curry, a nice yellow or white rice with all these accompaniments and none of the curry itself makes a good main dish. Children especially seem to like to pile raisins and peanuts on their rice. I usually also have Cipollini Onions (page 59), roasted asparagus, and this raita, or similar dishes. Add a big, crispy green salad, and everyone can find something to his or her liking.

2 teaspoons salt
2 teaspoons black pepper
1 cup all-purpose flour
4 whole boneless skinless chicken
   breasts, cut into chunks
3 tablespoons olive oil
2 large garlic cloves, chopped
2 large onions, chopped
1 cup heavy cream

2 cups (or more) chicken broth
1 tablespoon coriander
1/2 teaspoon cinnamon
1/2 teaspoon ground cloves
3 tablespoons (or more) cumin
1/2 teaspoon red pepper flakes or
   Tabasco sauce
Salt and pepper to taste

For Cucumber Raita, peel and shred 1 large English cucumber. Mix with 1 cup sour cream and 1 cup plain yogurt in a bowl. Stir in 2 teaspoons salt, 2 teaspoons pepper, and 2 teaspoons cumin.

Makes about 3 cups

Mix 2 teaspoons salt and 2 teaspoons black pepper with the flour. Coat the chicken with the mixture. Heat the olive oil in a large skillet. Add the garlic, onions, and the chicken in 1 or 2 batches to the skillet. Cook over medium heat until the chicken is cooked through. Remove to a large baking dish with a slotted spoon. Remove any remaining onions and garlic to prevent their scorching.

Add the cream, chicken broth, coriander, cinnamon, cloves, cumin, red pepper flakes, and salt and pepper to taste to the skillet. Cook over high heat for 5 to 8 minutes or until the liquid is reduced slightly, stirring frequently and scraping up any browned bits. Taste for seasonings. Add cumin if needed. Pour over the chicken in the baking dish.

Bake, covered with heavy-duty foil, at 350 degrees for 1 hour. Add more chicken broth if needed to prevent the curry from burning. Serve over yellow or white rice. Serve the Cucumber Raita (at right) on the side.

Serves 6

Chicken Enchiladas

2 tablespoons (or more) olive oil or vegetable oil
1 medium onion, chopped
3 to 4 green onions, chopped, with some of the green included
2 garlic cloves, chopped
1 small fairly mild pepper, such as banana pepper or Anaheim chile
6 boneless skinless chicken breasts, cut into strips
Salt and pepper to taste
1 tablespoon ground cumin
1 1/2 cups sour cream
1 cup chopped fresh cilantro .
6 (8-inch) flour tortillas
2 cups shredded Cheddar cheese
2 cups Blender Tomato Salsa (page 39)
3 small Roma tomatoes, chopped neatly
1 or 2 sprigs cilantro, for garnish

Heat the olive oil in a large skillet. Add the onion, green onions, garlic, and pepper. Sauté until wilted. Remove to a large bowl. Add more olive oil to the skillet if necessary. Sauté the chicken strips in batches until cooked through; do not crowd the skillet.

Mix each batch of chicken strips into the onion mixture in the bowl. Let stand until cool. Season with salt, pepper, and the cumin, and mix well. Taste and adjust the seasonings. Mix the sour cream, 1 cup cilantro, and additional salt and pepper in a bowl.

Use a slotted spoon (to remove excess liquid) to spoon the chicken mixture down the center of each tortilla. Top each with some of the sour cream mixture. Roll each tortilla, and arrange seam side down in a lightly oiled rectangular baking dish. Sprinkle each tortilla with cheese. Cover the baking dish with oiled foil.

Bake at 350 degrees for 30 minutes or until bubbly. Remove from the oven and spoon a wide strip of Blender Tomato Salsa down the center of the tortillas. Garnish with the chopped tomatoes and cilantro sprigs.

Serves 4 to 6

Blender Tomato Salsa

6 Roma tomatoes, chopped
1 small can green chiles, drained
1/2 cup coarsely chopped fresh parsley
1/2 cup coarsely chopped fresh cilantro
1 small sweet onion, coarsely chopped
2 garlic cloves, peeled
2 tablespoons ketchup
1 tablespoon vegetable oil
2 tablespoons cider vinegar

Combine all ingredients in a blender or food processor, and process until mixed well. If the tomatoes are too watery, strain the salsa to the desired consistency. If Roma tomatoes are not available, you can use 3 larger tomatoes, but you will need to peel them.

Makes about 2 cups

Black Bean Salsa

1 can black beans, drained
1 small Vidalia onion or other sweet onion, chopped
2 teaspoons Tabasco sauce
1 garlic clove, smashed
3 medium Roma tomatoes, chopped
1 tablespoon vegetable oil
1 tablespoon red wine or mild vinegar
2 teaspoons salt
1 tablespoon chopped fresh cilantro
1 to 2 teaspoons sugar
1 tablespoon cumin

Combine all ingredients in a bowl, and mix well. Let stand for 1 hour or longer. Taste and adjust seasonings. This recipe can easily be doubled.

Makes about 3 cups

Strudel with Creamed Chicken

3 tablespoons olive oil or vegetable oil
1 medium onion, chopped
3 medium potatoes, peeled, cooked, and cubed (about 3 cups cubes)
1 cup chopped fresh mushrooms
1 small garlic clove, chopped
3 ribs celery, chopped
1/2 cup chopped fresh parsley
3 cups cooked chicken, either chopped or pulled into bite-size pieces
2 teaspoons chopped fresh or dried tarragon
2 teaspoons dried thyme
Salt and pepper to taste
1 cup (or more) plain bread crumbs
Basic White Sauce (at left)
1 cup (2 sticks) unsalted butter, melted
1 cup plain bread crumbs
1 box frozen phyllo pastry, thawed

To make Basic White Sauce, melt 2 tablespoons unsalted butter in a skillet. Stir in 2 tablespoons all-purpose flour. Cook over medium heat, whisking constantly until blended and smooth. Whisk in 1 cup milk or heavy cream and 1 cup chicken stock. Cook for about 6 minutes or until the flour is cooked but not browned, whisking constantly. Season with salt and pepper to taste.

Makes about 2 cups

For the filling, heat the olive oil in a large skillet. Add the onion, potatoes, mushrooms, garlic, celery, and parsley. Sauté until the onion is wilted. Cook over high heat for 5 minutes longer or until all the liquid from the onion and mushrooms has evaporated. Add the chicken, tarragon, thyme, salt, pepper, and 1 cup bread crumbs. Add the White Sauce, and mix well. Add additional bread crumbs if the mixture will not hold its shape in a spoon. Taste and adjust seasonings. Let cool to room temperature.

For the pastry, have the melted butter, 1 cup bread crumbs, a pastry brush, and damp clean cloth ready. Open the phyllo package, and unroll it on the paper from the package, covering it with the damp cloth to keep the phyllo from drying out. Place 2 sheets of phyllo on a lightly oiled foil-lined 10x15-inch baking pan, brushing each sheet with butter. Sprinkle about 1 tablespoon bread crumbs on each sheet to keep them separate and thus flaky when baked. Continue layering 2 sheets at a time until there are 10 sheets in the stack.

Spoon a generous but neat cylinder of the filling down the center of the phyllo stack. Roll into a long cylinder, and tuck in the ends. Place seam side down in the baking pan. Brush with melted butter.

Bake at 375 degrees for about 40 minutes or until bubbly and golden brown. If the pastry browns too quickly, cover loosely with foil. Let stand for at least 10 minutes before serving.

Serves 4 to 6

Strudel, phyllo (or filo) dough, and phyllo pastry are all the same—a very thin pastry dough that, if handled correctly, can be very, very easy. Since it is so thin, it dries out and crumbles in a matter of minutes. After you remove it from the box, keep the heavy parchment-type paper around it as you unfold it. Keep a clean cloth or paper towel that has been dampened and wrung out somewhat over the thin sheets of dough as you work.

Have everything ready so that you don't give the dough time to dry out. You will need the damp cloth, a pastry brush or clean paint brush, a small bowl of melted unsalted butter, and a dish of crumbs (coarse plain bread crumbs for savory dishes, sweet crumbs such as graham cracker, cookie, or cake crumbs for desserts).

The crumbs are necessary when layering the phyllo dough to give enough space between sheets for the sheets to rise and not stick together during baking. This makes a much flakier product than just using the melted butter.

Be sure to thaw the unopened phyllo in the refrigerator the night before, because frozen dough will not behave itself, and you will hate it forever.

If you have leftover dried-out phyllo pieces without butter on them, save them in an airtight glass jar for bread crumbs. Freezing makes them soggy, and as long as they don't have butter on them, the crumbs will keep for weeks. (Buttered pieces will become rancid.) These are especially good with strudels, because in between the layers of phyllo, they cause each individual layer to puff up better than regular bread crumbs.

Vegetable Strudel

This recipe can be made in a traditional strudel shape by layering the first 5 sheets of phyllo on a lightly oiled foil-lined 10x15-inch baking pan, placing half the filling down the center of the dough and tucking in the ends of the dough, and then rolling it into a large, fat tube. Place seam side down in the baking pan, and brush with melted butter. Bake at 375 degrees for about 40 minutes. This recipe makes 2 strudel logs. Since the end pieces are mostly pastry and no filling, don't serve them. Just cut them off, and discard them.

2 tablespoons olive oil
1 medium sweet onion, chopped
4 ribs celery, chopped
3 garlic cloves, chopped
2 medium red bell peppers, julienned
1 medium yellow bell pepper, julienned
4 carrots, chopped
10 small fresh asparagus, trimmed and cut into 1-inch pieces
2 cups chopped fresh button mushrooms
1 cup fresh English peas, cooked until tender (optional)
1 cup fresh green beans, cooked until tender
2 cups artichoke bottoms, cooked and sliced into strips
Salt and freshly ground pepper to taste

1 (15-ounce) container ricotta cheese, nonfat ricotta cheese, or low-fat ricotta cheese
1 cup grated asiago, Parmesan, or Romano cheese, or a combination of the three
1 tablespoon fresh basil leaves, chopped
3 eggs, beaten
2 teaspoons salt
Freshly ground pepper
1 cup plain bread crumbs, if necessary
1 box frozen phyllo dough, thawed (see page 41 for directions on working with phyllo)
1/2 cup (1 stick) unsalted butter, melted
1 cup dry bread crumbs

Heat the olive oil in a large skillet. Add the onion, celery, garlic, bell peppers, carrots, asparagus, mushrooms, peas, beans, and artichoke bottoms, and mix well. Cook until the vegetables are wilted but still have some texture. Season with salt and pepper.

Mix all the cheese, basil, and eggs in a large bowl. Add 2 teaspoons salt and a few grinds of pepper. Remove the vegetables from the skillet with a slotted spoon. Stir into the cheese mixture. The mixture should be somewhat stiff; if it is too watery, add 1 cup bread crumbs.

Place 1 sheet of phyllo in a lightly oiled 10x13-inch baking dish, allowing the edges to come up the sides. Brush lightly with melted butter, and sprinkle with bread crumbs. Repeat until there are 5 layers. Spoon the filling onto the phyllo stack, spreading to all corners. Tuck the sides over the filling.

Fold 1 layer of phyllo carefully over the filling. Brush with melted butter, and sprinkle with bread crumbs. Repeat until there are 5 sheets of phyllo on top of the filling. Trim any ragged-looking dough with kitchen scissors, or tuck it into the sides. Brush the top with melted butter.

Bake at 375 degrees for 40 minutes or until the pastry is golden brown and the filling is bubbly. Cover with foil if the pastry darkens too quickly.

Serves 4 to 6

Spanakopitas, tiropitas, strudels, and all sorts of things are made with phyllo pastry. It can be made by hand, and most intensive pastry courses teach it. The quintessential statement about phyllo-making is, "You must roll it out thin enough to read a newspaper through each sheet of dough." Needless to say, it takes a very large work space and quick hands to roll out the dough yourself.

Ready-made fresh phyllo, which is often available in large cities, and the nationally available frozen phyllo are excellent products, and unless you are Greek and/or eat phyllo at every meal, you probably will be very happy with the frozen.

Phyllo is almost tasteless but is so flaky and adaptable that it adds a lot to otherwise ho-hum dishes. In our restaurant/cooking school days, Gwen Henry used to teach "Phyllo Phun" and other such catchy-titled classes, and despite their weird titles (my doing, not hers), her classes were very, very popular. She is an excellent cook and a great friend, and she taught us well. Maybe that's why so many of us enjoy phyllo dishes: a "remembrance" of our sweet friend Gwen.

Creamed Chicken and Biscuits

Technically, there is no baking to the chicken part of this recipe, but it is so good with biscuits that I am including it here. This is probably my personal favorite for breakfast. I make the best biscuits in the world, and their being very easy to make probably adds to my love for them. (The recipe is on page 88.)

I like the biscuits to be by the side of the creamed chicken, rather than the creamed chicken's smothering the biscuits. I serve it with small ramekins of fresh blueberries that I have cooked with 1 cup of sugar per carton of blueberries, 1 tablespoon grated lemon peel, and a vanilla bean. Cook just until the berries become soft and the sugar becomes a thin syrup. This is for the biscuits. Fresh Bing cherries work well like this, too, but they need a little more cooking than the tiny blueberries.

To make the Tarragon White Sauce, melt 3 tablespoons unsalted butter in a saucepan. Add 3 tablespoons all-purpose flour, whisking constantly until smooth. Whisk in 1½ cups chicken stock gradually. Whisk until smooth. Add 1 cup heavy cream and 1 tablespoon tarragon or thyme. Cook over medium heat for 5 to 6 minutes or until thickened and smooth, stirring constantly. Season with salt and pepper to taste. Add more cream or chicken stock if the sauce is too thick.

Makes about 3 cups

1 (4- to 5-pound) chicken
3 ribs celery, chopped
1 large onion, quartered
2 carrots, peeled and quartered
1 elephant garlic clove, chopped, or 2 small garlic cloves, chopped
1 cup chopped fresh parsley
5 or 6 peppercorns
1 tablespoon salt

1 cup dry white wine
Tarragon White Sauce (at left)
2 tablespoons olive oil, Tuscan if possible
1 pound fresh mushrooms, chopped
2 ribs celery, chopped
1 medium onion, chopped
Salt and freshly ground pepper to taste

Clean the chicken carefully, removing the liver and gizzard. Combine the celery, onion, carrots, garlic, parsley, peppercorns, salt, and wine in a large stockpot. Cover with hot water, and bring to a boil. Add the whole chicken carefully. Add additional boiling water if needed to cover the chicken. Reduce the heat. Simmer for 45 to 60 minutes or until the chicken is cooked through. Let cool slightly. Remove the chicken to a platter. Let stand until cool enough to handle.

Remove and discard the chicken skin. Debone the chicken, and return the bones to the stockpot. Leave the chicken on the platter; refrigerate if necessary while finishing the stock. Bring the stock to a rolling boil. Boil until reduced by half. Strain the stock into a bowl. Chill the stock, and skim off any fat that surfaces. Pull or chop the chicken into bite-size pieces. (You should have about 3 cups cooked chicken.) Mix the chicken and White Sauce in a bowl, and set aside.

Heat the olive oil in a skillet. Add the mushrooms, celery, and onion. Sauté until the vegetables are wilted. Season with salt and pepper. Add to the chicken mixture, and mix well. Taste for seasonings. Serve with biscuits.

Serves 6 to 8

To make everything come out at one time, I do what my Grandmother Oates taught me to do with pies whenever possible. Separately from the casserole filling, make the biscuits completely, but remove them from the oven when they have only another 5 minutes or so left to brown. Put the near-finished biscuits on the bubbling hot filling, and finish in a 350-degree oven for about 5 minutes. You can finish the biscuits to the browning point before putting them on the bubbling hot filling, and then all you have to do is keep the casserole warm in a 250-degree oven.

Cover it with foil if it begins to darken before you serve it.

My grandmother did this with almost all pies, and the filling and pastry were always perfect. It is especially helpful with fruit pies that are very juicy, because the pastry does not get soggy when it has been fully baked and then filled with the fully cooked cherry or peach filling.

Of course, you can serve fruit pies either warm or at room temperature. This method works especially well with puff pastry on the top of potpies. I bake the whole sheet of puff pastry on a foil-lined sheet pan until all the flaky layers are done. When I am ready, I get the potpie filling bubbling, then add the fully baked warm pastry. Then I cover it loosely with foil and keep it warm in the oven. You'll thank my Grandmother Oates and me for this. It's a real baking secret for success with pies.

Asparagus and Chicken Stew

Asparagus and Chicken Stew may sound like a strange main dish for breakfast or brunch, but it is wonderful with homemade biscuits and fresh cherry preserves. When I serve this on a buffet for breakfast or brunch, I have three medium-size glass bowls of three kinds of fresh fruit, rather than fresh fruit all mixed up in a fruit "salad." I have one bowl of sliced fresh oranges, one of sliced, sweetened strawberries, and one of sliced bananas in lemon juice and sugar (so they don't darken). Vanilla yogurt goes in a fourth smaller glass bowl. I add a big basket of toasted whole wheat breads, bagels, and the biscuits with butter, cream cheese, and whatever on the side. This menu is very colorful, but more than that, it ensures that everyone, especially the staunch traditionalist, gets something that he or she likes and recognizes for breakfast. I find that if staunch traditionalists find something they deem to be "safe," they are far more apt to try something new. Mornings are not good times to expect much of a sense of adventure from some of us.

1 pound fresh asparagus, washed and trimmed	3 tablespoons all-purpose flour
1/4 cup olive oil	2 cups (or more) any one or a combination of milk, cream, half-and-half, or skim milk
1 pound chicken breasts, lightly pounded	1 tablespoon fresh thyme leaves, or 1/4 teaspoon dried thyme
3 tablespoons olive oil	Salt and pepper to taste
1 tablespoon Dijon mustard	
3 tablespoons unsalted butter	

Arrange the asparagus spears on a foil-lined baking sheet. Drizzle with 1/4 cup olive oil. Bake at 350 degrees for 15 minutes or until the asparagus are tender-crisp. Remove from the oven, and let cool. Slice into 1/2-inch pieces, and set aside in a bowl.

Cut the chicken into thin strips. Heat 3 tablespoons olive oil in a deep sauté pan or Dutch oven. Add the chicken strips. Sauté until each piece is cooked through. Remove from the skillet, and set aside with the asparagus. Add the Dijon mustard to the sauté pan, and stir to loosen any browned bits. Pour over the chicken and asparagus.

Melt the butter in the sauté pan or Dutch oven. Add the flour, stirring until blended and smooth. Add the milk. Cook over medium heat for about 5 minutes or until the flour is cooked but not browned, whisking constantly. Add the thyme. Add the chicken mixture and the drippings from sautéing the chicken. Taste for seasonings.

This stew should be of medium thickness, so that it is not at all runny on the plate. Reduce the liquid if it is not thick enough, or add milk or cream if it is too thick. Serve hot.

Serves 6 to 8

This stew is excellent in Phyllo Cups. To make them, unwrap the thawed phyllo dough on a counter, leaving it on the paper in which it is packed. Cover any exposed dough with a damp cloth or paper towel. Using half the dough, cut it exactly in half width-wise all the way through to the heavy waxed paper. (If tightly wrapped, the other half will keep in the refrigerator for several days.) Cut it again so that you have four squares of phyllo. Have ready a lightly oiled muffin pan, melted unsalted butter, and a pastry brush or clean paint brush.

Layer 3 sheets of the dough in each muffin cup, brushing generously with the butter and sprinkling with about 1 tablespoon plain bread crumbs. Repeat the process once. Add a generous amount of cooked filling to each cup. Let the pointed edges stick up. Bake at 350 degrees for 20 minutes or until golden brown and bubbly. Cover loosely with foil if the pastry begins to darken too soon. I find that if the filling is very hot, it all turns out at the same time rather than if the filling is refrigerator-cold.

Makes 12 phyllo cups

Tortilla Breakfast Soup

In my first cookbook, Remembrances of Things Passed, *I recorded one of my favorite breakfast foods, Mushroom Barley Soup. It's a soup that I have never served "professionally" (that is, as a chef) for breakfast, but I keep it on hand for our house in the mountains. Now, this Tortilla Breakfast Soup shows how our lives and tastes have changed, especially over the last twenty years.*

In its own very different way, this soup is warm and comforting. We love having it in the mornings out on the porch, far away from the city, really relaxed and really hungry. Try it first for Sunday night supper, and then see how you feel about having the leftover soup on Monday morning. Frankly, it makes my Mondays much less foggy, and I hope it does yours, too. If so, you can triple this recipe with ease.

2 tablespoons olive oil
6 corn tortillas, cut into strips
Salt to taste
2 tablespoons olive oil
2 garlic cloves, chopped
1 small onion, chopped
4 green onions, chopped, with some of the green included
2 ribs celery, chopped
1 1/2 cups peeled and chopped tomatoes, undrained
3 tablespoons tomato paste
6 cups chicken stock
1 cup chopped fresh cilantro

1/2 cup chopped fresh oregano
1 tablespoon dried thyme
1 small jalapeño chile, seeded
3 cups cooked and shredded chicken
2 teaspoons salt
2 teaspoons freshly ground pepper
1 large avocado, cut into cubes
1 cup chopped fresh Roma tomatoes (about 6 to 8)
1 cup shredded Monterey Jack cheese or queso fresco
1 cup sour cream
1 lime, cut into thin slices

In my opinion, the toppings are very important to the success of this soup. For leftover soup, as described in the headnote, be sure to fry up some extra tortilla strips the night before, reserve some sour cream and shredded cheese, and, if you can, set aside an extra avocado for your Monday morning trial. Avocados don't keep very well outside of guacamole, and a whole small ripe one is easy to peel to garnish your soup with the next day.

Heat 2 tablespoons olive oil in a large skillet. Brown the tortilla strips in batches in the oil. Drain on paper towels. Season with salt while still hot.

Heat 2 tablespoons olive oil in the skillet. Add the garlic, onion, green onions, and celery; cook just until wilted. Add the tomatoes and tomato paste. Cook until the mixture begins to thicken, stirring constantly. Add the chicken stock, cilantro, oregano, thyme, and jalapeño chile. Cook over high heat for about 30 minutes or until the liquid is reduced by about 1/3. Discard the chile and any large pieces of herbs. Stir in the chicken. Season with 2 teaspoons salt and the pepper. Chill until serving time.

Divide the avocado pieces, Roma tomatoes, and some of the tortilla strips evenly among the soup bowls. Ladle the hot soup into the bowls; top with the cheese. Add 1 tablespoon sour cream and 1 lime slice to each serving. Serve any remaining tortilla strips on the side.

Note: Wear gloves to protect your hands when you seed the jalapeño.

Makes 6 servings

Chicken and Corn Bread Casserole

At truck stops in northern Alabama and Tennessee, a hungry diner gets big squares of corn bread with a lot of chicken gravy and some cooked chicken. It's a biscuits-and-gravy-kind-of-thing, but with corn bread. I find it hard to think, much less drive, after such a heavy meal, but the idea of corn bread and chicken really appeals to me. So, I modified it quite a bit, and I came up with a less soporific version. Mexican corn bread, which is corn bread seasoned with roasted peppers, green onions, and a bit of Tabasco sauce, makes a snappier version than this plain corn bread topping. Other corn bread recipes that can be used here are listed in the Index.

3 tablespoons vegetable oil or olive oil
3 tablespoons all-purpose flour
2 cups milk
1 cup chicken broth
1 tablespoon vegetable oil or olive oil
4 ribs celery, chopped
1 medium onion, chopped
2 garlic cloves, chopped or minced
1 tablespoon any one or a combination of thyme, tarragon, or cilantro

3 cups cooked chicken, cubed or pulled into bite-size pieces
Salt and freshly ground pepper to taste
1 cup cornmeal mix (Bisquick or other self-rising cornmeal mix)
1 egg, beaten
1/2 cup milk
1 tablespoon vegetable oil or olive oil
1 cup shredded cheese, such as Cheddar, Romano, Parmesan, fontina, or Monterey Jack

Heat 3 tablespoons vegetable oil in a large saucepan. Add the flour, whisking constantly until blended and smooth. Add 2 cups milk and the chicken broth all at once. Cook over low heat, whisking constantly until blended and smooth.

Heat 1 tablespoon vegetable oil in a skillet. Add the celery, onion, and garlic. Sauté until the vegetables are wilted. Add to the flour mixture, stirring to mix well. Add the herbs and chicken. Season with salt and pepper. Spoon into an ovenproof casserole.

For the corn bread, combine the cornmeal mix, egg, 1/2 cup milk, and 1 tablespoon vegetable oil in a bowl, and mix gently. Pour over the chicken mixture. Bake at 375 degrees for 45 minutes or until the chicken mixture is bubbly and the center of the corn bread is completely done. Spread the cheese over the top of the hot corn bread.

Serves 4 to 6

Grilled Pork Enchiladas

Usually, two small tenderloins come in a single package labeled "pork tenders." These are mainstays for chefs and home cooks. They are ready to roast or grill or cut into small medallions and sauté in very little time. Pork takes well to oriental seasonings (for example, sesame oil and ginger) or to any manner of barbecue and to a host of other equally delicious treatments. Here, the tenderloins are split almost in two, filled with Mexican-type herbs and spices, roasted or grilled, then sliced and rolled up into enchiladas. It can all be done a day ahead and reheated just before serving.

2 small pork tenderloins
Salt and pepper to taste
2 tablespoons olive oil
3 green onions, chopped, with
   some of the green included
1 can chopped green chiles,
   drained
1 teaspoon salt

1 teaspoon freshly ground pepper
1 teaspoon dried thyme
8 (8-inch) flour tortillas
Olive oil
3 small Roma or other plum-type
   tomatoes, chopped
Fresh cilantro, for garnish
Sour Cream Sauce (below)

Place the tenderloins on a lightly oiled foil-lined baking sheet with 1-inch sides. Butterfly the tenderloins lengthwise. Sprinkle with salt and pepper to taste. Combine 2 tablespoons olive oil, the green onions, green chiles, 1 teaspoon salt and 1 teaspoon pepper, and thyme in a small bowl, stirring until a paste forms. Spread down the center of each tenderloin. Bake at 350 degrees for 20 minutes or until the pork registers 170 degrees on a meat thermometer. Let stand until cool. Cut diagonally into thin slices.

Place some of the cooked pork on each tortilla. Roll each tortilla into a tube. Place seam side down in a lightly oiled ovenproof casserole. Drizzle with a small amount of olive oil. Bake, covered with foil, at 350 degrees for 30 to 40 minutes or until very hot. Remove the foil; top with the tomatoes. Garnish with cilantro. Serve the Sour Cream Sauce on the side.

Serves 4 to 6

Sour Cream Sauce

2 cups sour cream
4 green onions, chopped, with
   some of the green included
1/2 cup chopped fresh cilantro

3 small Roma or other plum-type
   tomatoes, chopped
Salt and freshly ground pepper
   to taste

Mix the sour cream, green onions, cilantro, and tomatoes in a bowl. Season with salt and pepper.

Makes about 2 1/2 cups

These enchiladas make a great late morning brunch menu or a summer supper. Add a green salad, and you're set. Vinaigrettes are easy to make, too, and there are so many wonderful vinegars on the market today that you can vary any salad merely by changing the vinegar. For this menu, a rather plain vinegar would be preferable to a fancier one ("fancy," such as balsamic, fig, or blood orange vinegar), because the enchiladas have so many flavors the fancy vinegar would be lost.

Vinaigrettes are usually three parts oil to one part acid (vinegar, lemon juice, etc.). Combine the vinegar and oil in a small glass jar with a reliable top. Add about a teaspoon of salt and freshly ground pepper, and shake vigorously. Use about 1/4 to 1/2 cup vinaigrette to approximately five cups lettuce. You can always add more, but drowning the lettuce ruins the salad. Add more lettuce if you do happen to overdo the vinaigrette. Toss well, and taste for seasonings. Too many salads are tasteless, when all they needed was the addition of the barest amount of salt.

Lamb Brodetto with Herbed Custard

Get a butcher, if you can find one, to trim and cut up a lamb leg for you to get the best lamb for stew. New Zealand lamb is excellent, but the lamb that I prefer is available at Jamison Farm in Latrobe, Pennsylvania. (See page 171 under Sources.)

The Herbed Custard is very pretty on top of this stew, but you can cover that with puff pastry if you like. Line an oiled 10x15-inch baking pan with foil, and place 1 sheet of puff pastry in the pan. Cut or stretch the pastry a little larger than your casserole (the pastry will shrink a little when baked). Vent the pastry with several decorative slices. Brush with 1 egg beaten with 1 teaspoon water. Bake at 400 degrees for 10 to 15 minutes or until the pastry is puffed and golden brown. Carefully remove the pastry from the pan, and place it on top of the Herbed Custard. Keep warm until serving time.

3 tablespoons olive oil or vegetable oil
4 pounds boneless lamb, cut into small cubes
1 large Vidalia onion or other sweet onion, chopped
3 cups chopped fresh button mushrooms
5 carrots, cleaned and cut into 1-inch chunks
3 ribs celery, chopped
2 sprigs of fresh rosemary, or 2 teaspoons dried rosemary
3 garlic cloves, chopped
1 cup (or more) beef broth or chicken broth
2 cups (or more) red wine
3 tablespoons tomato paste
Salt and freshly ground pepper to taste
Herbed Custard (sidebar, page 51)

Heat the olive oil in a large skillet. Brown the lamb in 3 batches, adding 1/3 of the onion with each batch. Remove each batch to an ovenproof casserole. Combine the mushrooms, carrots, celery, rosemary, and garlic in the skillet, and cook until the vegetables are wilted. Add the beef broth, wine, and tomato paste. Cook over high heat until reduced by half and somewhat thickened. Season with salt and pepper. Add to the lamb in the casserole, and mix well. The liquid should cover the lamb. Add more wine and/or broth if necessary. Cover tightly with foil and a heavy lid.

Bake at 350 degrees for 45 minutes or until the lamb is very tender and most of the liquid has cooked out. Be especially careful not to let it burn during the last 10 minutes or so. Remove from the oven, and carefully remove the lid and foil.

Pour the Herbed Custard carefully over the stew. It should be no more than one inch thick on top of the stew. Bake, uncovered, at 350 degrees for 15 minutes or until the center of the custard is done. (The baking will take a lot longer than 15 minutes if there is more than one inch of custard on top.) Be sure the stew is hot and bubbly when you add the custard and that you bake it immediately.

Serves 4 to 6

Brodetto is probably not the proper Italian name for this, but, like all Italian words, it sounds so melodic. Ancona and other towns near the Adriatic in Italy have a fish soup that is called brodetto, instead of the usual "minestrone." I like the idea of a lamb stew topped with the herbed custard and, to be totally American, topped with puff pastry.

My family thinks it should be called an "aria," instead of a "little broth," but would you really order an aria? Call it what you will, it is wonderful, especially at Easter, when we serve it with curried couscous and a mango chutney like Major Grey's. In Italy, mostarda di frutta is a type of spicy whole fruit accompaniment that we love. Some mostardas are very, very mustard-y and hot, but with time they cool off in their syrup. Get a mild one to begin with, unless you really like spicy hot things. Many mail order and online epicurean businesses have Italian mustard fruit. A cucumber and sour-cream-and-dill salad rounds out the perfect menu for lamb fans. You can substitute beef, and it will be just as good.

For the Herbed Custard, beat 4 eggs in a bowl. Add 3 tablespoons thyme, tarragon, fresh parsley, or chives. Add 1 teaspoon dried rosemary or 1 tablespoon fresh rosemary. Stir in 2 teaspoons salt, 2 teaspoons freshly ground pepper, 1 cup ricotta cheese, and 1 cup heavy cream, milk, or skim milk. Stir in 1 cup grated low-fat hard white cheese, such as Parmesan or asiago. Beat until smooth.

Makes about 3 cups

Lamb Curry

Be sure to get the best lamb that you can find. Butchers are more scarce these days than good lamb, but both are available. I have listed a wonderful lamb purveyor on page 171 under Sources, should you be at a loss for either a butcher or good lamb. For stew, which this recipe is, technically, I still use a good quality leg of lamb, boned and cut into very small cubes. I don't like what is generally sold as "lamb stew meat." I find it much too tough, even after long, slow cooking. The smaller pieces are easier to eat, especially on a buffet plate.

Oddly enough, restaurants in northern Italy frequently have wonderful curries. Harry's Bar in Venice, several very popular restaurants in the Milan area, and even a few in Rome serve excellent curries. Curries are easy to make, and they are always better when made ahead. I have given a number of alternatives in the Chicken Curry recipe on page 37, in case you are worried that not all your guests will share your enthusiasm for curry. For a lamb curry, I usually add a spicy tomato dish, which I have included here.

2 cups all-purpose flour
2 teaspoons salt
2 teaspoons freshly ground pepper
3 pounds boneless leg of lamb, cut into 2-inch cubes
3 tablespoons olive oil or vegetable oil
3 large garlic cloves, chopped or smashed
2 medium onions, chopped
4 ribs celery, chopped
3 cups red wine

3 tablespoons curry powder
1 teaspoon cinnamon
1 teaspoon ground cloves
2 cups peeled and chopped tomatoes, undrained
3 tablespoons tomato paste
1/2 cup brandy
4 cups chicken broth or beef broth
1 tablespoon salt, or to taste
1 tablespoon freshly ground pepper, or to taste (optional)

Mix the flour, 2 teaspoons salt, and 2 teaspoons pepper in a large zip-top plastic bag. Add the lamb, and shake until all the lamb is coated.

Heat the olive oil in a large skillet or Dutch oven. Add the lamb in batches to avoid overcrowding the skillet. Add some of the garlic, onions, and celery with each batch of lamb. Sauté until browned. Remove the lamb to a large baking dish.

For the sauce, add the wine to the skillet, after all the lamb has been removed. Stir with a whisk to loosen any browned bits. Add the curry powder, cinnamon, cloves, tomatoes, and tomato paste, and mix well. Cook over medium-high heat until the liquid is reduced by 1/3, stirring frequently until the sauce is smooth. Reduce the heat to low. Cook for several minutes, stirring occasionally.

Lamb Curry *(continued)*

Add a mixture of the brandy and half the chicken broth to the sauce, stirring constantly. Add the remaining chicken broth, and taste for seasonings. Season with the salt and pepper to taste. Stir in additional curry powder if desired.

Pour the sauce over the lamb pieces in the baking dish. Cover tightly with foil. Bake at 375 degrees for about 2 hours or until the lamb is very tender. Do not allow the liquid to boil out, especially near the end of the cooking time. Add additional chicken broth if needed. Serve with Spicy Tomatoes on Toasted Rounds (below), yellow or white rice, and any of the curry accompaniments listed with the Chicken Curry (page 37).

Makes 6 to 8 servings

Spicy Tomatoes on Toasted Rounds

2 tablespoons olive oil or vegetable oil
1 large onion, chopped
2 garlic cloves, chopped or smashed
3 ribs celery, chopped
5 cups peeled and chopped tomatoes, undrained
3 tablespoons tomato paste
Grated zest of 1 small lemon
Grated zest of 1 small orange
2 sprigs of fresh rosemary, each stuck into 1 lemon slice
1 teaspoon each cinnamon and ground cloves
2 teaspoons Tabasco sauce
2 teaspoons salt
2 teaspoons freshly ground pepper
2 long loaves French bread, cut into 1/4-inch slices and lightly toasted
1/4 cup olive oil

Heat 2 tablespoons olive oil in a large skillet. Add the onion, garlic, and celery, and cook just until wilted. Add the tomatoes and tomato paste, and mix well. Cook over high heat for about 20 minutes or until the mixture is quite thick. Add the lemon zest, orange zest, lemon slices, cinnamon, cloves, Tabasco sauce, salt, and pepper, and mix well. Chill in the refrigerator for several hours to overnight. Remove and discard the lemon slices and rosemary. Serve the spicy tomatoes with or on the toasted bread slices that have been brushed with 1/4 cup olive oil.

Makes 6 to 8 servings

Lamb and Phyllo Pie

Ground lamb for breakfast may sound a little rough to non-breakfast eaters, but eggs and cheese can seem a little weak on Sunday mornings after church. We have some missionary friends, Anne and Kemp Palleson, who used to visit with us from New Guinea years ago. Anne always said that after a long morning at church, everyone "has been good too long," and patience and more hearty fare were definitely in order.

Everyone does get more pleasant after lunch on Sundays, and I think Anne was onto something. My husband, a physician, said we were just hypoglycemic. Whatever. . . .

This is good especially around Easter, with a good green salad and a smile or two.

3 tablespoons olive oil, Tuscan if possible
1 large onion, chopped
1 elephant garlic clove, chopped, or 3 garlic cloves, chopped
3 ribs celery, chopped
1 pound ground lamb
1 pound ground round
2 teaspoons dill
1 cup plain yogurt
2 tablespoons tomato paste
Salt and freshly ground pepper to taste
1 box frozen phyllo dough, thawed (see page 41 for directions
   on working with phyllo)
1 cup (2 sticks) unsalted butter, melted
1 cup plain bread crumbs

Heat the olive oil in a skillet. Add the onion, garlic, and celery, and cook until slightly wilted. Add the lamb and ground round, and cook until completely browned. Let cool slightly. Add the dill, yogurt, tomato paste, salt, and pepper. Taste for seasonings; it should be very flavorful. Spoon into a baking dish.

Place 2 sheets of phyllo over the lamb mixture, brushing each sheet with melted butter. Sprinkle with 1 to 2 tablespoons of the bread crumbs. Repeat the process until there are 10 sheets of phyllo, tucking the edges in or trimming with a knife. The dough will shrink a little when baked.

Bake at 350 degrees until the filling is bubbly in the center and the pastry is golden brown. Cover loosely with foil if the pastry begins to brown too much.

Serves 6 to 8

Lobster for Breakfast!

Unlike many reunion groups, our original group of ten from our college days has stayed together rather well. Now, as then, we are all spread out in many different areas of the country. Each area is definitely unique and even somewhat exotic. We have met in Lexington, Kentucky, for the races; New Orleans for many occasions, since we went to Tulane; Chicago; and Charleston, South Carolina. Even the one who lives in the "country" lives on a genuine old plantation that is presently a horse farm amidst cotton fields. Two of us live in Birmingham.

Now, I ask you: What would you do for three days with ten fun friends when you don't have horses, cotton plantations, the French Quarter, the Garden District, or the Cubs? You get creative, that's what. And of course we had a wonderful three days. Birmingham has a lot to offer. To top it all off, we ended with a Sunday brunch at my house with Lobster for Breakfast!

2 eggs
2 cups milk
2 1/2 pounds fresh lobster meat, cut into bite-size chunks
2 cups bread crumbs
2 teaspoons dried thyme
2 teaspoons freshly ground pepper
3 tablespoons olive oil
2 large Vidalia onions, coarsely chopped
4 ribs celery, chopped

1 large garlic clove, chopped
6 cups (48 ounces) peeled and crushed tomatoes, undrained
2 cups dry white wine or chicken broth
2 teaspoons dried thyme
1 cup heavy cream
Salt and pepper to taste
3 drops of Tabasco sauce (optional)

Beat the eggs with the milk in a large bowl. Add the lobster, stirring until coated. Mix the bread crumbs, 2 teaspoons thyme, and the pepper in a large bowl. Add the lobster, stirring until each piece is breaded.

Heat the olive oil in a large skillet. Add the onions, celery, garlic, and lobster in batches. (Overcrowding the skillet will stew the lobster, rather than browning it, and will make it tough.) Sauté until the lobster is golden. Remove to a large flat ovenproof casserole. You can do ahead up to this point, add the cooled sauce (below), and refrigerate overnight. Then bake at 350 degrees just until the mixture is bubbly.

For the tomato sauce, combine the tomatoes and wine in the skillet, stirring to loosen any browned bits. Cook over very high heat for about 8 to 10 minutes or until the liquid is reduced by half. Add 2 teaspoons thyme and the cream. Cook over very high heat until the liquid is reduced by half and the cream is thick and almost browned. Let stand until cool. Taste for seasoning. Add the Tabasco sauce. Serve with cheese grits.

Serves 8 to 10

Cheese grits, roasted fresh asparagus, and a big green salad are great accompaniments for this tomato and lobster casserole. Just be sure no one in your crowd has shellfish allergies. You can substitute a good whitefish like scamp, grouper, or king mackerel for the lobster. You can even substitute chicken for the lobster, but you will have somewhat taken away the wow factor.

Pumpkin Baked in Its Shell

1 (8- to 10-pound) pumpkin
1 quart milk
2 cups heavy cream
2 tablespoons salt
1 cup shredded Cheddar cheese,
   mild, sharp, or mixed
1 tablespoon Tabasco sauce
1 tablespoon Worcestershire sauce
2 cups chopped cooked ham or
   smoked turkey, or a
   combination of the two

1 tablespoon olive oil
4 ribs celery, chopped
1 medium onion, chopped
2 green onions, chopped, with
   some of the green included
   (reserve some of the green
   for a garnish)
4 cups drained chopped tomatoes
2 tablespoons (or more) tomato
   paste
Salt and pepper to taste

The sweet version of this recipe as it was originally given to me needed a lot of help, so I added eggs and marsala (or sweet sherry, or nothing but vanilla), and pepped it up a bit in other ways. The white pumpkins are especially pretty with this custard, with dark grapes and some ivy or grape leaves surrounding the base of the pumpkin. They also help to cover the crumpled foil under the pumpkin. Pumpkins keep forever, so this would be good from fall almost until spring, when it's time to toss the pumpkins out back for the possums. Follow the recipe directions for cleaning the pumpkin and setting it on the foil. Place the pumpkin (on the foil) in a rectangular baking pan, and preheat it for 10 minutes at 350 degrees. The pumpkin should be quite hot when you add the custard.

➤

Cut the top off the pumpkin about 1/3 of the way down. Set aside to use as a lid. Scoop out and discard the fibers and seeds. The pumpkin must be very clean, but a thick wall is still necessary to keep it from collapsing during baking. Make a foil "X" with heavy-duty foil. Place the pumpkin in the center of the cross.

For the stew, bring the milk and cream almost to a boil in a large saucepan over medium heat. Add the salt, cheese, Tabasco sauce, Worcestershire sauce, and ham.

Heat the olive oil in a skillet. Add the celery, onion, and green onions, and cook until wilted. Let cool slightly, and stir into the cheese mixture. Stir in a mixture of the tomatoes and tomato paste. Taste for seasonings. Cook over high heat for 8 minutes or until the mixture begins to thicken. Add additional tomato paste 1 tablespoon at a time if necessary for thickening. You can prepare this part ahead, but bring it to a boil again before pouring it into the pumpkin.

Pour the hot tomato mixture into the pumpkin, and add its lid. Pull the foil around the pumpkin, and tighten the foil at the top. Place in a rectangular baking pan. Bake at 350 degrees for about 2 hours or until the mixture is almost the consistency of stew. The pumpkin should be cooked but not collapsing. (Crumple the foil around the bottom of the pumpkin to move it. Serve it on the crumpled foil, which will make a sturdier base and also keep the pumpkin warm.) Season with salt and pepper, and garnish with the reserved green onions.

Note: You can substitute lower-fat milk and low-fat cheese, but if you must omit the cream, then use a good beef broth or chicken broth, along with a little sherry or dry white wine. It will take a little longer to reduce it than it does with cream. Tomato paste will also help to thicken it without adding fat.

Serves 6 to 8

Virginia Johnson, my sister in Nashville, is, you will hear me say repeatedly, a much better cook than I am or ever have been. Actually, as time goes on, she is a better cook than I ever want to be. I'm tired a lot after raising three boys and running a restaurant. If I can cook it quickly, and somehow not manage to be just a mediocre cook, I'll gladly pin the blue ribbon on anyone else. My family and I are, indeed, "good little eaters," and we love to visit folks, especially Virginia (a.k.a. Gigi). She sent me a bunch of recipes whose notes were funnier than she is, and that's funny.

The recipe at left was not the one she intended for me to use. It was on a very, very frayed and yellowed page from a very, very defunct magazine (I think), and on it she had marked for me to try a hearth bread recipe that she had used for years. But, like all kitchen things are wont to be, the most torn and tattered recipe on the whole page was one for baking pumpkin in its own shell, something I have looked for for years. The ones I have tried always collapse and ooze all over my oven, and everyone says, "Are we supposed to EAT that?" which, of course, they never do. Here, stuck on the backside of Gigi's archives, is a real treasure of a recipe.

The one she gave me was a dessert custard, which is in the sidebar. I wanted a savory custard in a pumpkin, and I finally realized that a true custard precooked a bit like this one is, on top of the stove, and then finished in the oven in the pumpkin—ecco!—no oozing mess! Miniature pumpkins do work, but they are a nuisance to hollow out, because they are always so hard even if you bake them a little beforehand. And you need three per person for a one-cup-per-person serving. My favorites are the almost-white pumpkins that I get from a wonderful farmer on Sand Mountain, Alabama. They are all sizes, but the best ones are fairly small, maybe a pound or a bit more, and they are easy to hollow out.

For soup or a savory course, you can fill them about half-way, and that will be a good main course serving. For dessert, you could count two people to one 1-pound or larger pumpkin. The little orange and yellowish pumpkins work well, too. The 8- to 10-pound pumpkins that we normally see in the markets all fall are really the easiest to work with, and each pumpkin of that size will serve about four to six people. Do try to find pumpkins that have flat bottoms, because even a little bit of leveling with a knife on the bottom of an irregular pumpkin disturbs the fibers that will keep the pumpkin from collapsing during baking. My greengrocer tells me (every fall) that he's always looking for flat bottoms, too!

(continued)

Combine 1 quart milk, 3 cups whipping cream, 6 beaten eggs, 1 cup dark molasses (not blackstrap), 1/2 cup bourbon (optional), 2 teaspoons grated nutmeg, 2 teaspoons cinnamon, 2 teaspoons salt, and 1 tablespoon vanilla extract in a large saucepan. Bring almost to a boil over medium heat, stirring constantly. Reduce the heat, and boil until the custard almost coats a spoon; it will still be very runny. Pour into the prepared pumpkin. Bake at 350 degrees for 2 hours or until a knife inserted near the center comes out clean. (Test it at 1 hour. There are no generic pumpkins.) This will serve 4 to 6.

Noodle Pudding

Every few years, Kraft surveys consumers (that's us) for trends in individual and family buying and eating habits. Macaroni and cheese always leads the list of family favorites. An enormous percentage of consumers surveyed for the past ten years buys and eats boxed, frozen, or "from scratch" mac-and-cheese. An easy and slightly different take on this tradition is this Noodle Pudding, a very good "company" version of our favorite comfort food.

Any kind of cooked green vegetable can be added for taste and texture. Every age group in our family prefers fresh asparagus, cooked and cut into one-inch pieces, added to the pudding. Broccoli florets, zucchini slices, or a combination of these are very good, too, when fresh asparagus are too big and tough or simply not available. Any green vegetable should be cooked and bite-size. Vegetables that are too watery, such as zucchini, are better used in combination with other vegetables than by themselves. Spinach, too, must be drained and all the water pressed out carefully, or the pudding will not set. I put the cooked spinach in a very hot skillet all by itself, with no oil or anything else, and stir the spinach constantly for a few minutes to remove every drop of moisture. Be careful not to scorch it, though. The pudding is best with regular dairy products, but the low-fat or nonfat kinds are very good, too.

8 ounces cream cheese or nonfat cream cheese, softened
8 ounces ricotta cheese or nonfat ricotta cheese
6 eggs, beaten
2 cups milk or skim milk
2 teaspoons salt
2 teaspoons freshly ground pepper
2 teaspoons nutmeg
2 teaspoons Tabasco sauce
2 teaspoons vegetable oil
1 garlic clove, smashed or chopped

2 ribs celery, coarsely chopped
3 green onions, chopped, with at least 1 tablespoon of the green included
2 cups cooked and drained fresh asparagus, broccoli, spinach, and/or zucchini (cut into 1-inch pieces)
1 (8- to 10-ounce) package flat egg noodles, cooked and drained
2 teaspoons chopped fresh dill
1 cup sour cream, nonfat sour cream, or low-fat sour cream

Whisk the cream cheese, ricotta cheese, eggs, and milk in a large bowl until smooth. Add the salt, pepper, nutmeg, and Tabasco sauce.

Heat the vegetable oil in a skillet. Add the garlic, celery, and green onions; cook just until wilted. Mix with the cream cheese mixture. Stir in the asparagus and pasta. Spoon into a lightly oiled deep-sided ovenproof casserole. Bake at 350 degrees for about 1 hour or until a knife inserted near the center comes out clean.

Stir the dill into the sour cream. Unmold the pudding onto a platter. Top each serving with some of the sour cream.

Makes 6 to 8 servings

Cipollini Onions

Whenever there is a festivity of any sort at our house, I always plan to have these wonderful little Italian onions somewhere on the menu. I have often been accused of being a wanna-be Italian, and I am in a way. I always remind my accusers, however, that I am indeed an American. I was born on the Fourth of July, and I had an Uncle Sam. I never had a pony named Macaroni, but I have easily cooked my share of macaroni (pasta).

True cipollini can be troublesome to peel since they are so small. I have found that dropping all the little unpeeled onions into a pot of boiling water for no more than 3 or 4 minutes and then into a waiting bowl of ice water helps the skins to slip right off. Any more than 3 or 4 minutes in the boiling water would parboil the onions, and these are so sweet that parboiling is not necessary and actually makes them mushy.

Cipollini usually come in small mesh bags. For this recipe, you will need several of the little bags. If you can buy the onions loose, weigh out about 2 pounds or estimate about 4 or 5 cups of uncooked cipollini. I have found them to be so popular at our gatherings that I never seem to have enough. This recipe can be multiplied easily.

2 tablespoons good-quality
   olive oil
2 pounds cipollini onions, peeled
   (see headnote)
1/4 cup olive oil
1/2 cup (1 stick) unsalted butter
1 cup balsamic vinegar

2 cups (or more) chicken stock or
   beef stock
2 cups (or more) heavy cream
Salt and pepper to taste
1 cup grated hard white cheese,
   such as Romano or Parmesan

Heat 2 tablespoons olive oil in a large skillet. Add the onions, and sauté for about 3 minutes or until lightly browned. Remove to a baking dish.

For the sauce, add 1/4 cup olive oil, the butter, vinegar, chicken stock, and heavy cream to the skillet. Cook over high heat until the liquid is reduced by 1/3, scraping up any browned bits. This sauce should be very thick and dark. Season with salt and pepper.

Pour the sauce over the onions in the baking dish. Add more cream and/or chicken stock if the sauce does not completely cover the onions. You can prepare this dish ahead up to this point, and refrigerate until baking time.

Bake, tightly covered with foil, at 350 degrees for about 1 hour or until the onions are tender. The sauce will reduce to less than 1 cup, so be careful not to let the onions burn near the end of the baking time. Check occasionally before the hour is up, and re-cover with the foil to finish baking. Top with the cheese.

Makes 6 servings

Goat Cheese Spoon Bread

Spoon bread is more of a soufflé than a bread, despite its rather grainy texture. The cornmeal makes it more substantial-tasting than other soufflés. Since spoon bread, like soufflés, tends to be rather bland, it takes on flavors quite easily. Mixed with the spoon bread ingredients, the goat cheese appeals to a broader audience than you might think.

3 cups milk or part low-fat milk
1 cup yellow cornmeal, stone-ground if available
2 teaspoons salt
2 teaspoons Tabasco sauce
1 tablespoon Dijon mustard
16 ounces goat cheese, plain, herbed, or flavored
6 eggs, separated
2 teaspoons cream of tartar
16 ounces guava jelly, melted
3 tablespoons torn fresh mint (not chopped)

Bring the milk to a boil in a large saucepan. Add the cornmeal in a steady stream. Cook for 4 to 5 minutes or until the mixture begins to thicken, stirring constantly. Add the salt, Tabasco sauce, and Dijon mustard, and mix well. Add the cheese in small chunks, mixing well after each addition. Let stand until cool to the touch. Add the egg yolks, and mix well.

Beat the egg whites with the cream of tartar in a mixer bowl until soft peaks form. Lighten the egg yolk mixture with about 1 cup of the egg whites; then combine the two mixtures carefully. Pour into a greased 1-quart soufflé dish. Bake at 375 degrees for about 40 minutes or until a knife inserted near the center comes out clean. Just before serving time, heat the jelly with the mint leaves. Keep warm, and serve in a heatproof cream pitcher.

Note: This can be baked in 4 to 6 lightly oiled individual soufflé dishes (little ramekins). Then heat the mint and guava jelly. Just before serving, drizzle a circle or two on the top of each soufflé. The sauce will sink down into the spoon bread and become a real part of it. You could do this with the larger soufflé dish, but the hot guava sauce tends to wander through the cheese and cornmeal rather randomly, and that's not fair. It is so good on the spoon bread that I don't take a chance unless I'm using the little ones. You want everybody to get some of the sauce.

Makes 6 to 8 servings

My husband's family is from Florida, rare birds indeed, and we made the ubiquitous peanut butter and jelly sandwiches for all our three sons with guava jelly. Later in life, they realized this was not the normal pb&j, but by then, it was too late. We keep guava jelly like other people keep grape jelly. Guava jelly is also great on or in baked apple dishes, on curries, and in pies that call for glazes. There is a big difference in brands, and the better ones are usually from Florida.

$\mathcal{M}$y first cookbook, Remembrances of Things Passed, *was rather unorthodox in its format in that I wrote about the five decades of the Food Revolution, between 1940 and through the '80s, which just happened to be my own life span (thus far). In such a book, there were lots of recipes according to the five decades, but there were no traditional breads like corn bread, muffins, and rolls. I had not intended to wait almost ten years to write this book. Frankly, I had not intended to write it* ever, *but here I am enjoying every minute of it again. If recipes and cookbooks are in some magical way like Laura Esquivel's beautiful book,* Like Water for Chocolate, *then you must be laughing with all of us who had input on this book. Food stories to me are almost better than food itself—almost—well, a little.*

To succeed with food does take love in the kitchen like Esquivel says, and bitterness and rancor tend to mess up things in the soup as well as in our lives.

The best thing about writing and promoting Remembrances *was all the wonderful people I met, and especially all the wonderful "remembrances" people sent me from their own lives. Some people even sent photographs of me, of my friends and family, and of themselves, even if we had never met. These are such treasures, and I am afraid that our fast-moving lifestyles will rob us of their beauty, if not of their very existence, if we don't share them.*

The recipes in this section are all easy, delicious, and great to keep on hand or to give for gifts. There again, I think our fast-moving lifestyles have brought us to a real need for home-baked things. They still say to others that we care, and that is what it is all about.

It is important, however, for me to share the following e-mail I got from my friend Toby Sewell, as I began this chapter. Bear in mind that she has beautifully edited and directed two of the most elegant cookbooks published by a small press. Hers were through FRP in Nashville, Tennessee, the same company my friend Betty Sims and I both have used for our books, her Southern Scrumptious *and my* Baking Secrets.

"Subject: Righto. A new book. On Baking.

"Baking is a thing in my past. It is a frill (except for casseroles) when meat and potatoes are perfectly adequate. Actually, I used to bake all the time, and my French bread was in great demand. Never had a flop of any sort because I didn't know yeast was supposed to be temperamental. Then I went to a cooking demonstration of Betty's, and she said never let dough rise in a metal bowl (which I had been doing for about twenty years, quite successfully) and I haven't made a decent roll since then.

Sometimes knowledge is dangerous."

Baking Biscuits & Bread

for Dinners & Lunches

Contents

Coffee Can Bread

The nicest thing to me about coffee can breads is the nice round shape they make for tea sandwiches. When I was in the restaurant business, we had High Tea on Tuesdays, and we did a lot of off-premises catering as well. These round slices make great bases for any kind of open-face tea sandwiches. Toasted, they make wonderful bruschetta, which are open-face hors d'oeuvre similar to a small pizza. Since homemade bread dries out quite rapidly if sliced and left out in the air, lightly toasting the slices on a baking sheet in a 300-degree oven will make the bread dry enough to still be pleasant and, at the same time, keep the filling from making the bread soggy. Brush the toasted rounds with either melted unsalted butter or a very good olive oil for more flavor and crispness.

1 tablespoon yeast	2 teaspoons salt
1/2 cup warm water	1 tablespoon vegetable oil
3 tablespoons sugar	3 1/2 to 4 1/2 cups all-purpose flour
1 (12-ounce) can evaporated milk	

Dissolve the yeast in the warm water. Add the sugar, stirring until dissolved. Combine the evaporated milk, salt, vegetable oil, and yeast mixture in a large mixer bowl, and beat well. Add the flour 1 cup at a time, beating well after each addition. The dough should be pulling away from the side of the bowl and be quite sticky. Be careful not to add too much flour, which will make the dough dry.

Place the dough in a well-oiled 2-pound coffee can or two 1-pound coffee cans. Let rise for about 1 hour or until the dough almost reaches the top of the can. Bake at 350 degrees for 1 hour for the 2-pound can or 45 minutes for the 1-pound cans. Remove the loaves from the cans. Test for doneness by thumping the bottom of the loaf (it should sound hollow). Place the loaf on its side on a wire rack to cool. To store or freeze the loaf, return it to the coffee can, and cover it tightly.

Variations: For Light Wheat Bread, substitute 1 1/2 cups whole wheat flour and 3 cups all-purpose flour for the 3 1/2 to 4 1/2 cups all-purpose flour; replace the sugar with honey.

For Raisin Nut Bread, add 1 teaspoon cinnamon and 1 teaspoon nutmeg to the yeast mixture. Stir 1 cup golden raisins and 1 cup chopped pecans into the batter with the final addition of flour.

For Herb Bread, add 2 teaspoons dried dill, 2 teaspoons freshly ground pepper, and 2 teaspoons Tabasco sauce to the yeast mixture.

Makes one 2-pound loaf or two 1-pound loaves

These can be frozen when you first shape them and put them in the coffee cans (before the first rise). Cover the cans with their plastic lids or with oiled foil, and freeze until needed. Let thaw at room temperature. Bake the bread when the dough pops the lids off or when it has risen almost to the top of the can. They can be frozen for up to one month.

Cracked Wheat Bread

Donna Johnson developed the original of this bread years ago for her family. Sharon Campbell, the baker in our restaurant who followed Donna, multiplied the basic recipe times ten. We made it every day for our restaurant and for several others. It always smelled so heavenly in the early morning when I would pile big boxes of the loaves into my Honda Civic wagon. Some cold mornings there was so much bread in the car that the windows would steam up, and I would drive around enveloped in a heavenly fog.

4 cups boiling water
2 cups cracked wheat cereal
2 tablespoons salt
1 cup vegetable oil
1 cup honey
2 cups dark molasses
   (not blackstrap)

1/4 cup warm water
3 tablespoons yeast
6 cups (about) whole wheat flour
8 cups (about) unbleached white
   bread flour

Pour the boiling water over the cereal in the large bowl of a heavy-duty mixer. Add the salt, vegetable oil, honey, and molasses. Let stand until the cereal begins to swell and almost doubles in size, stirring occasionally. Mix the warm water and yeast in the measuring cup you used for the honey and molasses. Let stand until bubbly. Stir to dissolve the yeast. When the cereal mixture has cooled to about 100 degrees, stir in the yeast mixture. Beat with the flat beater until mixed well but not cold. Add the flours 2 cups at a time, beating well after each addition and scraping the bowl occasionally. You may not need all the flour. The dough should begin to leave the side of the bowl and cling to the beater.

Change to the dough hook. Knead for at least 8 minutes. The dough should be fairly sticky when you begin with the dough hook. You cannot over-knead it, but you can under-knead it.

Cover the bowl with a damp cloth, and let rise in a warm place for about 1 hour or until doubled in bulk. Punch the dough down, and knead again for 6 to 8 minutes. Shape into two 2-pound loaves or four 1-pound loaves. Place in well-seasoned oiled loaf pans.

Let rise for about 30 minutes or until doubled in bulk. Bake at 375 degrees for about 1 hour. If the dough begins to darken too soon, cover with a lightly oiled foil tent. Remove from the pans as soon as the bread is done. Place the loaves on their sides on a wire rack to cool completely. Do not slice for at least 1 hour. Bread this dense needs to finish its baking and cooling process uninterrupted.

Makes two 2-pound loaves or four 1-pound loaves

Dilly Bread

*Years ago, Gwen Henry and I went to Los Angeles for the annual meeting
of the IACP (International Association of Culinary Professionals). We
attended a class taught by Michael Roberts, who at the time had a
restaurant called Trumps. Michael was one of the kindest people we have
ever met, and a very generous chef. He was our single-most important
influence in establishing our High Tea at our own restaurant. Like his,
ours was a great success. I never got to tell him how much we appreciated
his help, his kindness, and his encouragement. I hope somehow he knows.*

2¹/2 cups all-purpose flour
¹/4 cup sugar
2 teaspoons baking powder
2 teaspoons salt
1 egg
¹/4 cup vegetable oil
¹/2 cup (or more) milk
1 tablespoon grated orange zest
1 tablespoon grated lemon zest
2 teaspoons curry powder
2 teaspoons saffron (optional)
2 teaspoons minced garlic
2 tablespoons finely chopped fresh dill, or 1 tablespoon dried dill

Mix the flour, sugar, baking powder, and salt at low speed in a large
mixer bowl. Lightly beat the egg and vegetable oil in a cup. Add the egg
mixture, milk, orange zest, lemon zest, curry powder, saffron, garlic, and
dill, and mix quickly. Mix in a bit more milk if the mixture is too dry. It
should look like cake or corn bread batter.

Place the dough in 2 well-oiled 1-pound coffee cans. (It will rise fairly
high in the oven, so do not fill the coffee cans more than ¹/3 to ¹/2 full.)
Bake at 300 degrees for about 25 minutes or until the loaves test done.

Makes two 1-pound loaves

*Michael baked this
wonderful quick
bread in a funny
little loaf pan called
a rehrücken
(pronounced "rare
rucken"). It is often
used in Viennese
baking, because it is a
subtle joke in Vienna.
A venison loin was
often served with
olives sticking up out
of it. It was a real
delicacy for the
Viennese royalty. Not
to be outdone, the
famous Viennese
pastry chefs made a
small chocolate cake
in the little fluted pan
and stuck the cake all
over with almond
slices to make it look
like a "loin" of
chocolate. It has never
struck me, or most
Americans, as being
droll, because I think
I would rather try to
make the venison loin
look like anything but
chocolate. How
disappointing to think
you were getting
chocolate, and you got
venison with olives in
it instead! Or even
vice versa. I like truth
in packaging, so I
bake this little dill loaf
in a one-pound coffee
can. It makes a nice
little compact loaf
that slices into nice
little rounds, and
that's what you
wanted in the first
place. Michael's was
cute, though, and of
course I went out and
bought the pan. I keep
paper clips in it.*

Oatmeal Yeast Bread

This dough, like most bread dough, can also be made into rolls. I have given a few of the different possibilities for roll shapes with the Basic Roll Dough recipe on page 81. Our granddaughter, Chloe, has a family nickname of "Clover," so we call cloverleaf rolls "Chloe rolls." She is already showing great promise as a baker, because she has so very, very much love to give. When her daddy, our Evans, was about four years old, he used to reply to us when we would say, "Evans, we love you," with "Well, it's mutal." That's how we feel about our Clover, too.

1 cup quick-cooking (not instant) oats
$1/4$ cup ($1/2$ stick) unsalted butter
$1/3$ cup packed dark brown sugar
2 teaspoons (rounded) salt
2 cups boiling water
2 tablespoons yeast
$1/2$ cup warm water
1 tablespoon sugar
4 cups all-purpose flour

Combine the oats, butter, brown sugar, salt, and boiling water in a saucepan, and cook for about 2 to 3 minutes or until the oats are swollen and cooked. Let cool to about 100 degrees. Dissolve the yeast in the warm water in a cup. Add the sugar to the yeast, stirring until dissolved. Combine the oat mixture and yeast mixture in a large mixer bowl. Beat at low speed until mixed. Add the flour 1 cup at a time, beating constantly and scraping the side of the bowl occasionally.

Let rise, covered with a damp cloth, for about 1 hour or until doubled in bulk. Punch down the dough. Knead the dough on a lightly floured surface until the dough is elastic and not at all sticky. Shape into two loaves and place in well-oiled loaf pans. (Or shape into rolls and bake as described on page 81.)

Let rise, covered, for about 30 minutes or until doubled in bulk. Bake at 350 degrees for 45 to 60 minutes or until the loaves test done.

Makes 2 loaves

Semolina Bread

Many people associate semolina with cornmeal, but in America it is, by definition, wheat flour. Semolina is a "hard" wheat with a very high protein content. It is most often used in pasta; in breads it needs the addition of some bread flour in order to make a more tender loaf. For breakfast and lunch, semolina bread is wonderful with any of the egg dishes, but it is also excellent with soups and salads.

1 tablespoon yeast
2 teaspoons sugar
$1^1/_2$ cups warm water
2 cups semolina flour
2 teaspoons salt
2 to 3 cups (about) all-purpose flour
3 tablespoons olive oil

Dissolve the yeast and sugar in the warm water in a large mixer bowl, stirring occasionally. Add the semolina flour and salt. Beat at low speed until a batter forms. Add 1 cup of the all-purpose flour, beating at medium speed until mixed. It is better to knead the flour in at medium speed than to use too much flour. Kneading or mixing with the flat beater of a heavy-duty mixer will make the dough moist but not sticky. Add more flour, if necessary, 1 tablespoon at a time; beat well after each addition. Let stand, covered, for about 1 hour or until doubled in bulk.

Punch down the dough. Shape into loaves similar to French bread baguettes. Place on a well-oiled heavy baking sheet. Let rise for 30 to 45 minutes or until doubled in bulk. Brush the top of each loaf with the olive oil.

Bake at 400 degrees for 25 to 30 minutes or until the loaves are golden brown and can be moved around easily on the baking sheet.

Makes 2 loaves

Sourdough Bread

Years ago, when I closed my restaurant and bakery, I felt so exhausted that I had few regrets, if any. It did cross my mind that I should have brought my sourdough starter home with me. It was in a huge glass jar in the reach-in refrigerator. We had kept it going for years. I cannot imagine what the people who bought the reach-in thought it was. It is easy to start another one, because "a little leaven leavens the whole lump." You can keep this starter going if you keep it in a tightly covered large glass jar in the refrigerator and feed it once a week with a mixture of 1 cup bread flour and 2/3 cup water. If you make a lot of sourdough, you can feed the starter every third day.

1 tablespoon yeast	1 tablespoon salt
1 tablespoon sugar	1/2 teaspoon baking soda
1 3/4 cups warm water	7 to 7 1/2 cups (about) bread flour
1 cup Sourdough Starter	

Dissolve the yeast and sugar in the warm water in a large mixer bowl, stirring occasionally until foamy. Add the Sourdough Starter, and mix well at low speed. Add the salt, baking soda, and 1 cup of the flour at a time, mixing well at low speed and scraping the bowl occasionally. Beat at medium speed until the dough is shiny and leaves the side of the bowl. Let rise, covered, for about 1 hour or until doubled in bulk. Punch down the dough. Shape into 2 loaves; place each loaf in a well-oiled loaf pan. (Or, you can bake it free form. Shape the dough into 2 rounds; place them on foil-lined baking sheets.) Let rise for about 45 minutes or until doubled in bulk.

Bake at 400 degrees for 10 minutes. Reduce the oven temperature to 350 degrees. Bake for 45 minutes or until golden brown. Remove from the pans; let cool for at least 1 hour.

Makes 2 loaves

Sourdough Starter

1 tablespoon yeast	1 1/2 cups warm water
1 tablespoon sugar	1 1/2 cups bread flour

Begin the starter four or five days before you will be using it. Dissolve the yeast and sugar in the warm water, and mix well. Let stand until foamy. Add the flour gradually, mixing well after each addition. Refrigerate until needed.

Makes about 2 1/2 cups

Easter Egg Twists

Sharon Campbell was a "real" chef who worked with us in the restaurant business. The rest of us were not. In fact, our motto was, "We don't know what we're doing, but we're getting better at it." Enter Chef Sharon, and we experienced an extra measure of God's grace. Sharon was an honors graduate from the Culinary Institute of America. We reaped a lot of benefit from her expertise and her quiet, diligent, kind ways. To say we loved her is an understatement.

Her Easter Egg Twist was my all-time favorite. I had never seen anyone put whole, colored raw eggs in raw dough before. It makes perfect sense, though, because the eggs bake along with the bread, and everything comes out at once.

15 raw Grade A extra-large eggs
1¹/₂ cups sugar
2 tablespoons yeast
1 tablespoon salt
1¹/₄ cups milk
¹/₂ cup (1 stick) unsalted butter, melted
6 cups (or more) all-purpose flour
4 eggs, beaten

1 cup golden raisins
1 cup slivered or sliced almonds, toasted
1 tablespoon anise seeds
1 egg
1 tablespoon water
Glaze (at right)
1 pound sweetened coconut
1 pound jelly beans

Dye 15 eggs using Easter egg dye. Set aside. Combine the sugar, yeast, salt, milk, and butter in a mixer bowl. Add the flour, 4 eggs, raisins, almonds, and anise seeds. Beat at medium speed until the dough is glossy and pulls away from the side of the bowl. If the dough is too sticky, add 1 cup (or more) flour gradually.

Divide the dough into six 12-inch ropes. Twist 2 ropes together into a figure 8, stretching as needed so that you have 3 large, tight ropes.

Nest 5 dyed eggs per figure 8, placing their fatter side up: 2 in the top loop of the 8, 1 in the middle, and 2 in the bottom loop. Push them in gently; don't break them.

Let rise in a warm place until doubled in bulk. The eggs should be securely in place, but push each egg down gently to be sure they stay secure. Beat 1 egg with 2 tablespoons water. Brush the mixture over each loaf. Place on a lightly oiled foil-lined 10x15-inch baking pan. Bake at 375 degrees for 45 minutes or until the loaves test done. Let cool completely.

Using the glaze as "glue," make a nest of coconut in the loops of each 8. Fill with jelly beans.

Makes 3 large loaves

To make the "glue" glaze, combine 1 pound confectioners' sugar, 1 cup milk, and 1 tablespoon vanilla extract in a bowl. Stir until a pourable paste forms.

Brioche, the Queen of Breads

Brioche, the delicious, rich, eggy French bread, is, for many bakers, the hallmark of their baking abilities. The reason for that is more likely to be because of its very dramatic appearance, rather than because of its difficulty to bake. Its appearance is, indeed, grand: The classic brioche has a lovely topknot that crowns its lovely fluted sides. At its simplest, it is a lovely little oval of fragrant, golden bread.

2 tablespoons yeast
1/2 cup (or more) warm water
1 tablespoon sugar
4 to 5 cups all-purpose flour, sifted
6 eggs, beaten
1 tablespoon salt
1 1/4 cups (2 1/2 sticks) unsalted butter, softened
1 egg, beaten
2 tablespoons water

Dissolve the yeast in the warm water in a cup. Add the sugar, stirring until dissolved. Combine 1 cup of the flour and the yeast mixture in a large mixer bowl. Beat at medium speed, adding a bit more water gradually if needed to make a stiff gray paste. Continue beating at medium speed until a stiff gray dough forms. Place the dough in a lightly oiled bowl. Cut a deep X into the entire lump to open it up to room temperature. Let stand, lightly covered, until the X is entirely open and the lump has doubled in size.

Combine 3 cups of the flour, 6 eggs, and the salt in a large mixer bowl. Mix with the dough hook at low speed for 3 to 5 minutes or until blended. Add enough of the remaining flour gradually to make a stiff but not dry batter. Add the softened butter 1 tablespoon at a time, blending well after each addition and scraping the side of the bowl occasionally. Beat at medium speed for several minutes.

Beat the risen dough into the egg mixture with the dough hook at medium speed for at least 8 minutes, until there is no gray showing. Cover with a damp warm cloth, and let rise until doubled in bulk. A long, slow rise in the refrigerator will produce a beautiful cake-like crumb, but you can hurry the process somewhat without sacrificing too much texture by letting it rise at room temperature for about 1 1/2 hours. In the refrigerator it will take about 24 hours to rise.

Brioche *(continued)*

Punch down the dough. Knead on a lightly floured surface several times. It should be easier to work with after its first rise, and it should be glossy and not very sticky.

Shape as desired. The classic shapes are small fluted brioche pans or large 1-quart pans. To form the classic brioche, shape the dough into balls about half the size of a tennis ball. The dough is so buttery that there is no need to oil the brioche pans unless they are new and unseasoned; in that case lightly oil them, and wipe away any excess oil. Rather than rolling a small ball and sticking it to the main one, use sharp scissors to cut around the top of the ball in the brioche pan, releasing a little topknot. Do not cut it completely free of the main ball of dough. Give it a little twist to keep it from returning whence it came in the second rising.

Place the pans in a sturdy 10x15-inch baking pan. Cover loosely with lightly oiled waxed paper. Let rise until almost doubled in bulk. The small ones will rise in about 30 minutes; the large ones in 40 minutes or so. Brush each brioche gently with a mixture of the beaten egg and 2 tablespoons water.

Bake at 375 degrees until golden brown and not at all doughy. The wonderful fragrance should tell you that they are done. If they begin to darken before they are fully baked, cover the entire baking pan with a tent of lightly oiled foil.

Makes about 12 small brioche or 2 large ones

Typically, brioche is topped with sugar after it cools, because in France it is usually served as a breakfast bread. Brioche, however, makes the world's best sandwich and tea bread, toasted or plain. Classically, brioche uses what is known as a "levain," which is French for "leavening." The "levain" is allowed to rise separately from the batter; then it is beaten into the batter, after its first rise, to leaven the entire lump. It always sounds rather Biblical to me, because "a little leaven," indeed, "leavens the whole lump."

Quick, or 'Mock,' Brioche

This version, which I am sure tempts you far more than the classic version, is an excellent product. It is a little easier to make than the preceding recipe. After you are convinced that you can make this mock brioche, give the original classic one a try. You, too, will be a fan of this wonderful bread.

2 tablespoons yeast
$1/4$ cup warm water
1 tablespoon sugar
$1^1/2$ cups buttermilk, at room temperature
3 eggs, beaten
$3/4$ cup ($1^1/2$ sticks) unsalted butter, softened
$1/3$ cup sugar
2 teaspoons baking powder
1 tablespoon salt
$5^1/2$ to 6 cups all-purpose flour, sifted
1 egg
2 tablespoons water

Dissolve the yeast in the warm water in a cup. Add 1 tablespoon sugar, stirring until dissolved. Pour the buttermilk into a large mixer bowl. Add the yeast mixture, 3 eggs, the butter, $1/3$ cup sugar, the baking powder, salt, and $2^1/2$ cups of the flour. Beat at low speed for 3 to 4 minutes or until well mixed.

Change to the dough hook. Add the remaining flour gradually, beating constantly at medium speed until the dough pulls away from the side of the bowl and becomes slightly glossy. Do not add more flour than necessary. Knead at medium speed for about 5 minutes or until the dough is shiny and only slightly sticky. You cannot over-knead the dough.

Shape the brioche as desired and place in individual fluted brioche pans. Cut the topknot and twist lightly, but do not detach the little topknot from the brioche.

Place the brioche pans in sturdy 10x15-inch baking pans. Let rise for about 10 minutes for the small ones, 20 minutes for the larger ones. Beat 1 egg with 2 tablespoons water in a cup. Brush over the brioche.

Bake at 400 degrees for 5 minutes. Reduce the oven temperature to 375 degrees. Bake until the brioche are golden brown, fragrant, and not at all doughy, about 8 to 10 minutes for the smaller ones and up to 25 to 30 minutes for larger ones in loaf pans.

Makes about 24 small brioche or 2 bread pan loaves

Irish Soda Bread in Orange Syrup

John, our middle son, was almost born in Ireland. My husband, Bill, and I went to Ireland with a group of physicians and dignitaries from Jacksonville, Florida, when I was about 11 months pregnant with John (so it seemed). Bill's father paid for Bill's trip, and my dear precious mother came to my rescue and paid my way. We were poor as poor could be, since Bill was only a resident at Charity Hospital in New Orleans. We were elated to be going anywhere, especially on a private jet. It certainly was exciting enough for me to get up and go, even in my "delicate condition."

The physicians on the trip were obstetricians on holiday, too; and they made a wide berth around me until the return trip, when they realized I probably would make it home without a brand-new Irish citizen of my own in tow. (There is no group more dangerous to be around than a group of vacationing surgeons. They will either kill you running for you or, more likely, while running from you.) Thankfully, great recipes and wonderful memories were all the "extras" that I brought home. Irish Soda Bread is one of them. John came a month later.

1 cup whole wheat flour	2 teaspoons cardamom
1 cup (or more) all-purpose flour	Grated zest of 1 lemon
1/2 cup rolled oats	(about 1 tablespoon)
1 1/2 teaspoons baking powder	1 cup golden raisins
1/4 teaspoon baking soda	6 tablespoons unsalted butter,
2 teaspoons salt	melted
2 teaspoons caraway seeds	1 egg, beaten
2 teaspoons nutmeg	1 cup yogurt or low-fat yogurt

Mix all the flour, oats, baking powder, baking soda, salt, caraway seeds, nutmeg, and cardamom at low speed in a mixer bowl. Add the lemon zest and raisins, and mix quickly. Mix the butter, egg, and yogurt in a bowl. Add 1/3 at a time to the flour mixture, beating just until mixed after each addition.

Pat the dough into two large round loaves. The mixture should be stiff enough to stand on its own. Knead in a bit more all-purpose flour if needed to make a nice shape. It should still be quite moist, though. Place each loaf in a well-oiled and lightly floured 8-inch round baking pan. Cut a shallow X in the top of each loaf with a very sharp knife.

Bake at 375 degrees until each loaf sounds hollow when tapped on the bottom. Place the loaves on a wire rack to cool. Pour the warm Orange Syrup (at right) over the bread.

Makes 2 loaves

For the Orange Syrup for this bread, mix 1 cup fresh orange or tangerine juice with 1 cup sugar in a small saucepan. Bring to a boil over medium-high heat. Boil until the sugar is dissolved and the mixture begins to become syrupy, stirring constantly. Do not boil for longer than 10 minutes, or the mixture will crystallize. Watch carefully to keep it from boiling over.

Lemon Tea Bread

Sometimes you come across a recipe that just seems like your new best friend. In the early '80s, my sister, Virginia, gave me a little cookbooklet from an herb farm in Tennessee. This quick bread was in among a lot of wonderful treasures. Over the years, however, I have really enjoyed the Lemon Tea Bread the most of all the treasures in that little typed booklet.

In the restaurant/takeout business during that same decade, we sold these little loaves by the hundreds. We ate them ourselves by the gazillions. I still give them for presents, especially in the summers, when lemon thyme seems to be growing everywhere. It used to be a rare herb, so we learned to substitute for it. This tea bread works with lemon verbena and plain thyme, too, but the light delicate flavor of lemon thyme is best. Decorate the tops of the breads with more fresh sprigs of lemon thyme and a few bachelor buttons if you have them, and you'll have some new best friends yourself. Don't we all need those?!

Lemon thyme is fairly easy to find in garden shops these days, and it does not take much to get a big patch growing. Resist the temptation to either over-water it or even feed it, because it does well on its own. Also, this batter can be made into pretty little cakes, a real passion of mine. Little loaf pans, little heart-shaped pans, fluted brioche pans, baba cups, corn bread stick pans: the possibilities are endless. My favorite suppliers are listed on pages 170–171 under Sources.

Be sure to adjust the baking time accordingly, especially with little pans that are not very sturdy, such as baba molds. I lower the baking temperature for baba molds to 325 degrees, and bake them for about 6 to 8 minutes or until they test done. This recipe can be divided in half for making the smaller cakes, but use only 1 scant teaspoon of baking powder if so.

2¹/₄ cups milk
3 long sprigs fresh lemon thyme,
    or 1 tablespoon dried thyme
6 cups all-purpose flour
2 teaspoons baking powder
2 teaspoons salt
1 cup (2 sticks) unsalted butter,
    melted

3 cups sugar
Grated zest of 2 large lemons
6 eggs, beaten
2 cups (about) confectioners'
    sugar
Juice of ¹/₂ lemon (about)
Sprigs of fresh lemon thyme,
    for garnish

Heat the milk in a saucepan. Add the lemon thyme and remove from the heat. Let steep for at least 20 minutes. Remove and discard the lemon thyme.

Combine the flour, baking powder, and salt in a large mixer bowl, and mix thoroughly but quickly. Combine the butter, sugar, lemon zest, eggs, and milk in a bowl, and mix well. Add to the flour mixture, and beat at the lowest speed just until mixed; do not overmix. Spoon into lightly oiled and floured loaf pans.

Bake at 350 degrees for about 40 minutes or until the center of the loaf tests done. Place the loaves on their side on a wire rack to cool.

Place the confectioners' sugar in a bowl. Add the lemon juice gradually, mixing with a fork until a fairly thick paste forms. It may not take much juice. Let stand for at least 10 minutes to thicken before spooning over the loaves. Adjust the confectioners' sugar and lemon juice accordingly. The glaze should be highly visible when poured over the cooled bread. Garnish with sprigs of lemon thyme.

Makes 3 loaves

Donna's Sweet Bread

Donna Johnson baked these sweet rolls for our restaurant every Wednesday night. She is so diligent that she would often come into the shop during the night to check on her dough, especially this one. It was always perfect. Maybe all that diligence paid off, but I have mixed it up, popped it in the refrigerator at home, and slept like a baby while it did its thing in the fridge, and I've never had any trouble with it, either.

1 cup sour cream
1/2 cup sugar
1 teaspoon salt
1/2 cup (1 stick) unsalted butter, melted
2 tablespoons yeast
1 cup warm water

2 eggs, beaten
4 cups all-purpose flour
16 ounces cream cheese, softened
3/4 cup sugar
1 egg, beaten
1/2 teaspoon salt
2 teaspoons vanilla extract

For the dough, heat the sour cream in a saucepan over low heat. Stir in 1/2 cup sugar, 1 teaspoon salt, and the butter. Let cool to lukewarm. Sprinkle the yeast over the warm water in a large bowl; stir until dissolved. Stir in the sour cream mixture, 2 eggs, and the flour. Cover tightly; refrigerate overnight.

For the filling, beat the cream cheese, 3/4 cup sugar, 1 egg, 1/2 teaspoon salt, and the vanilla in a mixer bowl until light and fluffy. Cover and refrigerate overnight.

Divide the dough into 4 equal portions. It will be quite sticky. Roll 1 portion into an 8x12-inch rectangle, 1/4 inch thick, on a floured board. Spread 1/4 of the filling on the rectangle, leaving a 1-inch space on each side. Roll into a tube from the wide side; pinch closed. Place seam side down on a lightly oiled baking sheet. Repeat with the remaining dough and filling. Let rise for 30 minutes or until almost doubled. (It will finish rising in the oven.) Just before baking, make 3 or 4 diagonal slashes in the top of each loaf to let the heat reach all the way to the bottom of the loaves. Do not slash along the sides, or the filling will ooze out while baking.

Bake at 375 degrees for about 25 minutes or until the loaves are golden brown and baked all the way through. Be careful of the hot filling when removing from the oven.

Let stand for at least 1 hour before slicing. Refrigerate or freeze if you will not be using all the bread in one day.

Makes 4 large loaves or about 36 small loaves

This dough can be made into individual filled buns instead of the four large ones. I think you get more of the wonderful filling with the individual ones, but the large ones are a lot easier to shape.

When we were in the restaurant business, we took this recipe and multiplied it by ten, and we had no problem with it. I haven't done that myself in years, so I can't advise you. If you feel driven to such heights, I don't think you will regret it. As I recall, it worked every time for us. You will need a heavy-duty mixer, a commercial oven, and a very good, big refrigerator.

Cheesy Walnut Bread

This is a basic roll mixture all gussied up in a lovely shape. It is beautiful on a buffet for a brunch or lunch, but especially on a supper buffet. Grits and scrambled eggs can be quite perked up by the textures and flavors in this bread. Ignore the olives if you or your audience can't stand them, but I think they add enough flavor and pizzazz that I would give it a try, even with little guests. They just may surprise you in their acceptance if you don't call it "olive bread," which it could rightfully be named.

2 tablespoons yeast
$1/2$ cup warm buttermilk
2 eggs, beaten
$1/2$ cup sugar
1 tablespoon salt
$3/4$ cup vegetable shortening
1 cup boiling water
$3/4$ cup cold water
$3/4$ cup chopped walnuts
$3/4$ cup sliced green olives
$3/4$ cup shredded Swiss cheese
5 cups (about) all-purpose flour
2 cups shredded Cheddar cheese
$1/3$ cup sour cream
2 tablespoons chopped green olives
3 slices bacon, crisp-cooked and crumbled

Dissolve the yeast in the buttermilk. Stir in the eggs, sugar, and salt.

Combine the shortening and boiling water in a large mixer bowl. Beat at low speed until the shortening is completely melted. Add the cold water. (This will bring the mixture to about 100 degrees and won't kill the yeast when it is added.) Add the yeast mixture, and mix well. Add the walnuts, $3/4$ cup olives, and the Swiss cheese. Add the flour 1 cup at a time, beating well after each addition. You may not need all the flour. Beat at medium speed until the dough becomes shiny and begins to leave the side of the bowl, scraping the bowl occasionally. Let stand, covered, for about $1 1/2$ hours or until doubled in bulk.

Punch down the dough. Shape into a thick 18-inch roll, and place in a well-oiled large bundt pan or 10-inch tube pan. Let rise for about 1 hour or until doubled in bulk.

Bake at 325 degrees for 40 to 45 minutes or until the loaf sounds hollow when thumped on the bottom. Remove from the pan. Place the loaf on a wire rack to cool.

Combine the Cheddar cheese and sour cream in a blender, and process until blended. Stir in 2 tablespoons olives. Spoon into a bowl, and sprinkle with the bacon. Serve with the bread.

Makes 1 loaf

Apple Walnut Bread

Quick breads are those baked without yeast as a leavening agent. In order to give quick breads some rise, or texture, usually leavening agents such as baking powder and/or baking soda are used. The quick bread here is actually better if made the day before and reheated: A real boon for early morning breakfasts or brunches, especially.

1 cup coarsely chopped walnuts
3/4 cup (1 1/2 sticks) unsalted butter, softened
1/2 cup vegetable oil
2 eggs
2 1/2 cups all-purpose flour
1 tablespoon sugar
1 teaspoon salt
1 teaspoon baking soda
1 teaspoon baking powder
1 cup buttermilk or sour cream
1 tablespoon Dijon mustard
2 medium apples, coarsely chopped
8 ounces bleu cheese, such as Roquefort or Maytag

Spread the walnuts on a foil-lined baking sheet. Bake at 325 degrees just until they begin to darken. Remove from the oven, and set aside.

Beat the butter and vegetable oil in a large mixer bowl until fluffy. Beat for 3 to 4 minutes longer, scraping the bowl occasionally. Add the eggs one at a time, beating well after each addition. Beat at high speed for about 4 to 5 minutes or until the curdled look is smoothed out.

Mix the flour, sugar, salt, baking soda, and baking powder together. Add the flour mixture and buttermilk alternately to the egg mixture, mixing well after each addition. Mix in the Dijon mustard.

Stop the mixer, and add the apples, toasted walnuts, and cheese. Beat at low speed just until mixed; do not overbeat. Pour the batter into a well-oiled loaf pan. Bang the pan on a hard surface to level the batter in the pan (I use the floor).

Bake at 350 degrees for 1 hour or until the bread tests done at the center. Cool in the pan for 10 minutes. Remove to a wire rack to cool completely.

Makes 1 loaf

This quick bread is wonderful for breakfast served with guava jelly. It is also excellent as an open-face sandwich with smoked turkey or baked ham. Instead of using the traditional loaf pan, very small cake pans (2x3 1/2-inches) make beautiful little breads to serve in a basket. This recipe makes about one dozen of the very small breads. See pages 170–171 under Sources for the little cake pans.

Monkey Bread

Gloria Hampe, an ubermom if ever there was one, used to make this routinely for gatherings. Somehow, mine never tasted as good as hers. It must be her sweet, kind spirit coming through again. I try, I really do, but she is a loving, generous person, and a wonderful friend. (Now I can call her to bake it for me again.)

If you freeze the unbaked loaves immediately after shaping them into bubble loaves, they cannot have their second rise until later. In my opinion, this makes a better product, because the yeast gets a longer, slower, colder rise. Form the bubble loaves in the pans, brush with the melted butter, and freeze them immediately, uncovered at first.

If you need your tube pans before finishing the loaves, you can remove the frozen loaves from their pans, wrap them very tightly with plastic wrap and then heavy-duty foil, label them, and use your pans.

To thaw and bake the bread, place the unwrapped frozen loaves in lightly oiled and floured tube pans, cover with a warm cloth, and let rise at room temperature until doubled in bulk. This may take as long as 3 or 4 hours, depending on your room and your freezer temperatures. When they have doubled in bulk, bake as directed.

1 medium baking potato, peeled and cubed
2 cups boiling water
2 tablespoons yeast
2 tablespoons vegetable oil
1 cup milk

1/2 cup sugar
6 cups all-purpose flour
2 teaspoons (rounded) salt
1/2 cup (1 stick) unsalted butter, melted

Cook the potato in the water in a saucepan until tender. Remove the potato with a slotted spoon; reserve 1 cup of the cooking liquid. Mash the potato, and set aside. Let the cooking liquid cool to about 100 degrees. Add the yeast. Let stand until bubbly, stirring to dissolve the yeast. Stir in the vegetable oil.

Combine the mashed potato, milk, and sugar in a large mixer bowl. Add the yeast mixture; mix gently with the paddle attachment. Add 2 cups of the flour, and beat for about 5 minutes. Let rise, covered with a damp warm cloth, for about 2 hours or until doubled in bulk. Mix the remaining 4 cups flour with the salt. Add 1 cup at a time to the potato mixture, beating at low speed after each addition; scrape the bowl occasionally. Do not add more flour than necessary; the dough should not be dry. Beat with the paddle attachment until the mixture begins to leave the side of the bowl. Beat at medium speed for 4 to 5 minutes longer, changing to the dough hook if necessary.

Remove the dough to a lightly floured surface. Divide into 2 long rolled tubes. Line the tubes up parallel to each other. Cut the tubes into 2-inch lengths with a dough cutter or flat spatula. Roll each into a ball. Make 2 rows of balls in each of 2 well-oiled 10-inch tube pans, leaving a 1-inch space between the balls. (You can freeze the dough at this point; if so, see the sidebar for baking instructions.)

Let rise until doubled in bulk. Bake at 400 degrees for 15 minutes or until the middle bubbles are golden brown and done. Brush the rolls with the melted butter just before removing from the oven so that the bubbles brown thoroughly. If the bubbles have gotten too brown, butter them after removing from the oven. Let cool slightly, and remove from the pans. Place on a wire rack to cool (so they don't get soggy in the pans).

Makes 2 bubble loaves

Basic Roll Dough

1$\frac{1}{3}$ cups milk
$\frac{1}{3}$ cup sugar
2 teaspoons salt
$\frac{1}{2}$ cup vegetable oil
2 tablespoons yeast

$\frac{1}{2}$ cup warm water (105 to
 115 degrees)
2 eggs, beaten
7 cups all-purpose flour, sifted

Bring the milk, sugar, salt, and vegetable oil just to a boil in a medium saucepan, stirring to dissolve the sugar and salt. Let stand until lukewarm, about 90 to 95 degrees. Dissolve the yeast in the warm water, stirring occasionally.

Combine the milk mixture, yeast mixture, and eggs in a large mixer bowl, and mix well. Add 1 cup of the flour at a time, beating at low speed with the paddle attachment after each addition. Continue adding flour 1 cup at a time and beating at low speed until the dough begins to pull away from the side of the bowl and becomes shiny but not at all sticky.

Knead at medium speed for about 5 to 6 minutes, changing to the dough hook if necessary. Let rise, covered, for about 1 hour or until doubled in bulk. Punch down the dough, and shape into rolls as directed below.

For Pan Rolls, place biscuit-size balls of dough in a 9-inch round baking pan. The balls should not touch. Let rise. Bake at 400 degrees for about 15 to 20 minutes or until golden brown.

For Parker House Rolls, pat out the entire batch of dough. Roll into a circle 1 inch thick. Cut with a biscuit cutter or small empty tuna can (cleaned, of course), brush with melted butter, and fold over into pocket books (purses). Pinch together to hold their shape while baking. Place on a baking sheet. Let rise for about 30 minutes. Bake at 400 degrees for about 15 to 20 minutes or until golden brown.

For Cloverleaf Rolls, roll the dough into a long fat tube (like a hot dog). Cut into 2-inch lengths, and roll each into a small ball. Place each ball in a well-oiled muffin cup. Use sharp scissors to cut an X into the top of each ball, cutting almost to the bottom of the ball. The X will open into four corners while baking. Let rise for about 20 to 30 minutes or until doubled in bulk. Bake at 400 degrees for about 15 to 20 minutes or until golden brown.

Makes about 2 dozen rolls

Basic Roll Dough #2, Large Batch

Gigi, my sister in Nashville, sent me this 1960s recipe, which is a wonderful basic dough for either bread or rolls. It is a very large yeast recipe that can be used for dinner rolls or for pecan, orange, or other sweet rolls. It can even be shaped and baked into a loaf for bread. The original recipe was from Mrs. Somebody-I've-never-heard-of, and at the bottom of the recipe, Gigi wrote: "She's dead now. She was quite nice."

4 cups milk
1 cup vegetable oil
1 cup sugar
2 tablespoons yeast
8 cups all-purpose flour
1$^1/_2$ tablespoons salt

Bring the milk, vegetable oil, and sugar just to a boil in a saucepan, stirring until the sugar is dissolved. Let cool to about 100 degrees. Add the yeast, and mix well. Pour into a large mixer bowl. Add a mixture of the flour and salt 1 cup at a time, mixing well after each addition. Beat until the dough is completely mixed and beginning to pull away from the side of the bowl.

Let rise, covered, until doubled in bulk. Punch down the dough. Remove to a lightly floured surface and shape as desired as described on page 81.

Note: You can divide this dough in half and freeze part of it. Let it thaw, covered, overnight in the refrigerator. Then let it rise at room temperature until doubled in bulk. Punch it down, and shape as desired.

Makes about 4 dozen rolls

This large batch recipe differs from the other one in that there are no eggs added to the batter. Thus, this eggless batter makes a basic roll dough that keeps in the refrigerator for a day or so, can be frozen, and is a little simpler to mix than the Basic Roll Dough (page 81). Eggs in the dough do make a much richer-tasting roll, but I doubt if you will miss them in this second recipe.

Pecan Cinnamon Rolls

Some of the savory casseroles in Chapter 1 of this book really need the texture of these rolls. Texture is extremely important in the satiety rate of foods. How lovely that we can add texture to real treats like cinnamon rolls! Don't tell the nutritionists or the food police, or they will set us straight about their ideas about satiety-rate foods. I don't think I want a whole lot of broccoli or carrots here; pecans will do just fine, even in buttery, yeasty sweet rolls!

1 recipe Basic Roll Dough (either recipe, page 81 or 82)
1 cup packed brown sugar
1 cup all-purpose flour
1 cup chopped pecans or other nuts, such as walnuts, almonds, or
   macadamias
1/4 cup (1/2 stick) unsalted butter
2 teaspoons cinnamon
2 teaspoons nutmeg
2 teaspoons cardamom (optional)
2 teaspoons salt

Shape the dough into two (or more, see sidebar) 7x14-inch oblongs. For the filling, combine the brown sugar, flour, pecans, butter, cinnamon, nutmeg, cardamom, and salt in a bowl, and mix until a stiff paste forms. Spread about 1 cup of the filling in a neat tube down the center of each oblong. You should have about 1/3 of the oblong covered with filling. Adjust the amount of filling accordingly.

Roll each oblong into a tight tube, pinching the sides together to prevent the filling from leaking during baking. Brush each lightly with butter, and place on a lightly oiled foil-lined 10x15-inch sheet pan. (Or, cut each oblong into 1-inch slices, and place the slices in well-oiled muffin cups.) Let rise for about 20 to 30 minutes. (They will finish rising in the hot oven.)

Bake at 375 degrees for about 35 to 40 minutes for the loaves or 20 to 30 minutes for the rolls.

Makes 2 to 4 oblongs or 2 to 4 dozen rolls

Either of the Basic Roll Doughs gets quite billowy when it is all risen. Really slap it down on your work surface to get the air out of the dough, or cut it into two or more large sections to make it easier to wrestle around if you are just not up to it. Small sections work quite well, and you will be more apt to use this recipe if you don't find it too daunting the first time.

Each oblong section should have about 1/3 of its total as filling. Leave the edges of the oblong clear of filling, roll into a tube, then pinch the edges together and tuck them under slightly to keep the filling in during baking. Place the oblongs seam side down on a lightly oiled foil-lined baking pan with small sides. You can make rolls just as in the main recipe here instead of the tubes.

Cheese Madeleines

Marcel Proust's Remembrance of Things Past *certainly inspired the title of my first cookbook,* Remembrances of Things Passed. *But because of the unorthodox nature of my book (it covered five decades of the "food revolution"), there was no section for breads. No madeleines in a book remotely recalling Proust!*

To make up for it, here are some very unorthodox madeleines: bleu cheese and dill. Proust's, of course, were buttery sweet, and they can be found in any good French baking book. Arrange these in a large circle with their little shells on the outside. Sprinkle them with more cheese just before serving.

Madeleine pans come in several sizes. The large ones are the easiest to bake, but you will have to double the recipe for a dozen. Be sure that you have sprayed the pans with a good nonstick coating. If you don't, the cheese will cause them to stick. Corn bread baked in these pans is good for soup and/or salad suppers, too.

1/4 cup (1/2 stick) unsalted butter, softened
4 ounces bleu cheese, such as Roquefort or Maytag
16 ounces cream cheese or low-fat cream cheese, softened
1/2 cup sour cream
1 tablespoon Dijon mustard
2 teaspoons Tabasco sauce
3 eggs, beaten
1 cup all-purpose flour, sifted
2 teaspoons dill
1 teaspoon salt
1 teaspoon freshly ground pepper
3 tablespoons grated Parmesan or Romano cheese

Combine the butter, bleu cheese, cream cheese, and sour cream in the bowl of a heavy-duty mixer, and beat until blended and smooth. Add the Dijon mustard, Tabasco sauce and eggs, and mix well.

Mix the flour, dill, salt, and pepper together. Add to the cheese mixture, and stir just until mixed. Spoon into well-oiled madeleine pans, filling the pans about 1/3 full. Bang the pans on a hard surface to settle the batter.

Bake at 400 degrees for about 8 to 10 minutes or until the madeleines are puffed and golden brown. Arrange in a large circle with their shells on the outside. Sprinkle each madeleine with Parmesan cheese.

Makes 2 dozen medium madeleines

Ginger and Orange Marmalade Muffins

If you don't care for orange marmalade like we do, you can substitute lemon, lime, grapefruit, or three-fruit marmalade. Orange marmalade muffins, however, have a wonderful affinity for eggs and bacon or ham. If you don't have too large a crowd, you can make these muffins in the smaller muffin cups and fill them with sliced baked ham or smoked turkey.

This used to be quite popular when Martha Stewart had her catering business in the early 1980s. If she could go to all that trouble, so could we. Be forewarned: Slicing the muffins and filling them, and keeping their tops and bottoms from separating in the serving basket, can be tricky. A little softened butter helps to glue the two muffin pieces together, but I have still seen a very jumbled up basket of muffin pieces when they start to come apart. It works nicely, however, with a very small crowd.

1$\frac{1}{2}$ cups (3 sticks) unsalted butter, softened
1 cup sugar
3 eggs
Grated zest of 1 small lemon
3 cups all-purpose flour
2 teaspoons salt
2 teaspoons ginger
1 tablespoon (scant) baking powder
$\frac{1}{2}$ cup milk
8 ounces orange marmalade, melted
1 cup packed brown sugar, sifted

Oil 12 paper muffin liners, and place them in muffin cups. Set aside.

Cream the butter and sugar at high speed in a mixer bowl until light and fluffy. Add the eggs and lemon zest, and beat for about 5 to 6 minutes or until blended and smooth.

Mix the flour, salt, ginger, and baking powder together. Add the flour mixture and the milk alternately to the creamed mixture, beating just until mixed after each addition. Do not overmix, or the muffins will be tough. Stop the mixer, and add the melted marmalade; mix well.

Spoon the batter into the prepared muffin cups. Bake at 350 degrees for 20 to 25 minutes or until the muffins test done. Let cool for 10 minutes. Sprinkle each muffin with brown sugar.

Makes 12 muffins

Peanut Butter and Jelly Muffins

Serve these wonderful muffins with coffee in the mornings or with tea any time. Children tend to prefer grape jelly, of course, but those jams and jellies that are more tart than grape are especially good. Some tart jams and jellies include quince, lemon marmalade, ginger marmalade, red currant, and mild pepper jelly.

$2/3$ cup chunky peanut butter
2 eggs
1 cup milk
$1^1/2$ cups all-purpose flour
$1/2$ cup cornmeal
$1/4$ cup sugar
2 teaspoons baking powder
1 teaspoon salt
$1/3$ cup jam or jelly

Oil 12 paper muffin liners, and place them in muffin cups. Set aside.

Beat the peanut butter and eggs at medium speed in a mixer bowl for about 5 minutes or until they are well mixed and not at all curdled looking. Add the milk and mix well, scraping the side of the bowl occasionally. Beat at medium to high speed for about 6 minutes or until smooth.

Mix the flour, cornmeal, sugar, baking powder, and salt together. Add to the peanut butter mixture gradually, beating at low speed until mixed and scraping the side of the bowl occasionally. Do not overbeat once the flour has been added, or the muffins will be tough.

Spoon the batter into the prepared muffin cups. Place 1 tablespoon jam in the center of each muffin, pressing the tablespoon down into the muffin to make a well with the jam. Bake at 375 degrees for 20 to 25 minutes or until the center muffin tests done.

Makes 12 muffins

Three-Bear Muffins

The wonderful San Diego Zoo used to name their bears berry names. Among them were Razz Bear, Blue Bear, Boysen Bear, Straw Bear, and Huckle Bear. These muffins are almost as memorable, and certainly any one of those "bears" will do here.

3 cups flour
2 teaspoons baking powder
1 teaspoon salt
$1/2$ teaspoon baking soda
$1^1/2$ cups sugar
2 eggs, beaten
1 cup (2 sticks) unsalted butter, melted
1 cup fresh strawberries, sliced into quarters
$1/2$ cup fresh raspberries
$1/2$ cup fresh blueberries or blackberries
2 tablespoons sugar
2 tablespoons cinnamon

Lightly oil 12 paper muffin liners, and place them in muffin cups. Set aside.

Combine the flour, baking powder, salt, baking soda, and $1^1/2$ cups sugar in a large bowl, and mix well. Add the eggs and butter, stirring just until mixed; do not overbeat. Add all the berries at once, and mix by hand.

Spoon the batter into the prepared muffin cups. Bake at 375 degrees for 20 to 25 minutes or until the muffins test done.

Let cool for 10 minutes. Mix 2 tablespoons sugar with the cinnamon, and sprinkle evenly over the muffins.

Makes 12 large muffins

Biscuits

Years ago, Eleanor Henderson and I went to Atlanta to Nathalie Dupree's cooking school at Rich's. Both Nathalie and Rose Berenbaum were teaching, and Eleanor and I got a real overload that weekend. One of the many things that have stayed with me the strongest over the years are the biscuits that a woman who worked for Nathalie made for us every day.

Her name was Kate, and she was not very communicative, so Eleanor and I watched her every single time she made biscuits to see if we could find out why they were so heavenly. Shirley Corriher, a wonderful food scientist, was also there, and she took pity on us and told us the "secret": a wet, wet dough, she said, and a hot, hot oven. Her wonderful, indispensable book, Cookwise, gives a lot more explanation than that, and I don't know how cooks, but especially bakers, get along without it.

This biscuit recipe is adapted from what we saw from Kate and from Shirley's book. I have doubled it here and made a few changes. There are not many changes to make, though, to something this simple.

Our youngest son, an M.D./Ph.D., loves Shirley's erudite book. He'd love her, too, and her Arch Corriher. I miss those days and those friendships. Our lives have moved so fast and so far, but a good plate of biscuits helps to soothe somewhat the homesickness I feel for all those wonderful friends.

3 cups self-rising flour
1/2 teaspoon salt
1/4 teaspoon baking powder
2 tablespoons sugar
6 tablespoons Crisco vegetable shortening (the stick form is easiest)
2 cups heavy cream
1/2 cup buttermilk
Unsalted butter

Oil and lightly flour two 9-inch round baking pans; set aside. Mix the flour, salt, baking powder, and sugar in a bowl with your hands or a pastry blender. Add the shortening by tablespoonfuls until it is almost incorporated. There should be very visible pea-size pieces of shortening. Add the cream and buttermilk, and mix quickly with your hands or a small spatula.

Pull off dough the size of the biscuits you want and, with floured hands, quickly shape into balls. Place them in the pans with their sides touching. Handle them quickly.

Bake at 425 degrees for 10 to 15 minutes or until the center biscuit is golden brown and springs back when lightly touched. Place pieces of unsalted butter over the hot biscuits.

Makes about 3 dozen biscuits

A few years ago, when I worked for a bed-and-breakfast, I would make these biscuits up the night before without the liquids. In the morning, I would stumble into the dark, cold kitchen, add the cream and buttermilk, mix them quickly, fire up the ovens, shape the biscuits, and put them in their pans. They would then hold in their pans while I got everything else ready. Ten minutes before the crowd came in to eat, I would pop the biscuits in the oven.

I usually made three double batches every morning for 15 people, regardless of what else I served. People raved! These biscuits are superb! I used either guava jelly, whole cherry preserves, or mild pepper jelly, and, of course, the tops of the biscuits were dripping with butter.

I have frozen them, shaped and unbaked, for friends' emergencies (weddings, funerals, etc.), but the moisture dissipates a bit, and that's what makes them so fluffy, I think. They are best fresh, if possible. These are the biscuits I use baked on top of my Creamed Chicken (page 44).

Sweet Potato Angel Biscuits

"Angel biscuits" are biscuits leavened with yeast. The yeast adds a nice texture to biscuits with other ingredients, such as cheese or nuts or, as here, sweet potatoes. These biscuits, filled with a bit of pepper jelly, slivered ham, or smoked turkey, are wonderful for cocktails, too.

2 tablespoons yeast
3/4 cup warm milk
7 to 8 cups all-purpose flour
1 1/4 cups sugar
1 tablespoon baking powder
1 tablespoon salt
1 teaspoon cinnamon
1 teaspoon nutmeg
1 teaspoon freshly ground pepper
1 1/2 cups shortening (Crisco in sticks is the easiest)
Juice of 1/2 lemon
3 cups cooked sweet potatoes, mashed

Combine the yeast and warm milk. Let stand until the yeast is bubbly. Stir until smooth.

Mix the flour, sugar, baking powder, salt, cinnamon, nutmeg, and pepper in a large mixer bowl. Add the shortening by tablespoons, beating at low speed after each addition and scraping the side of the bowl if needed. Stir in the yeast mixture. Mix thoroughly but quickly.

Stir the lemon juice into the sweet potatoes. Add to the flour mixture. Beat at low speed for about 5 to 6 minutes or until the mixture leaves the side of the bowl. Let rise, covered, until almost doubled in bulk.

Punch the dough down. Roll it into a long, fairly thin tube on a lightly floured surface. Cut the tube into 1-inch slices. Place on an oiled foil-lined baking sheet. Let rise until almost doubled in bulk. Bake at 400 degrees for about 10 minutes or until the middle biscuit tests done.

Note: These biscuits freeze nicely at almost any point after the first rise. Let them come to room temperature to rise, then proceed according to the directions above.

Makes about 4 dozen biscuits

Anadama Bread

Not for one minute do I believe that this wonderful cornmeal bread was developed and named by an irate husband married to a woman named Anna. Just ask Laura Esquivel, who wrote the beautiful book Like Water for Chocolate, *and she will tell you nothing good comes from swearing at your food. Personally, I think it's just a misunderstanding of the word "anagram," which, loosely translated, means "to sort of mix things up." Anyhow, this is a wonderful bread; just be sure to stir a lot of kindness into it, and you can't fail. Hopefully.*

2 cups boiling water
$1/2$ cup plain cornmeal, white if possible
$1/2$ cup dark molasses (not blackstrap)
1 tablespoon salt
1 tablespoon unsalted butter, melted
1 tablespoon yeast
$1/2$ cup warm water
1 teaspoon sugar
$4^1/2$ cups all-purpose flour

Pour the boiling water over the cornmeal in a large bowl, and mix well. Let stand for about 1 hour. The cornmeal will swell as it cools off.

Mix the molasses, salt, and butter in a bowl. Add to the cornmeal, and mix well.

Combine the yeast, warm water, and sugar in a large mixer bowl. Let stand until foamy. Set the mixer at very low speed. Add the cornmeal mixture, and beat slowly but thoroughly with the paddle attachment. Change to the dough hook. Add the flour 1 cup at a time, stopping once the dough is somewhat sticky and begins to climb the dough hook. Let stand, covered with a warm damp cloth, for about 1 hour or until doubled in bulk.

Punch down the dough. Shape into two neat loaves, and place each loaf seam side down in a well-oiled 1-pound loaf pan. Let rise for 1 hour or until doubled in bulk.

Bake at 350 degrees for about 1 hour or until the loaves fall easily out of the hot pans and sound hollow when thumped on the bottom. Remove from the pans. Place the loaves on their sides on a wire rack to cool.

Note: Bread is always better if allowed to cool at least 1 hour before slicing. Slice with a serrated knife.

Makes 2 loaves

Corn Bread

There are as many ways to cook corn bread as there are cooks to cook it. There really is no "right way," and I don't care who tells you that or where they are from: North, South, or whatever. Corn bread can be sweet if it goes on spicy barbecued meats; it can be quite flat and bland if it is to be topped with chicken hash; and it can be downright hot if it goes with Mexican foods.

My mother always made hers on top of the stove in a small cast-iron skillet that was never washed (just wiped out a little so it stayed seasoned). Then the cake was turned with the browned side up and run into the oven for the last few minutes of cooking.

A hot, hot skillet, often with some oil or fat and a sprinkling or two of cornmeal to fry a bit before the batter goes into the skillet, adds a lot of crunch and texture to the corn bread.

Muffin tins and corn bread sticks in their special pans (and, of course, Mother's small skillet) were usually cast-iron. Cast-iron, a big household item in our iron-ore-laden Red Mountain area, was as ubiquitous as a kitchen fork at one time. Now, they are hard to find, harder to keep seasoned because of their lack of use, and yet still beloved.

2 cups plain cornmeal
1/2 cup all-purpose flour
1/2 cup sugar (or less, depending on where you're from)
2 teaspoons baking powder
2 teaspoons salt
1 teaspoon baking soda
2 cups buttermilk
1/2 cup melted shortening

Mix the cornmeal, flour, sugar, baking powder, salt, baking soda, buttermilk, and shortening in a bowl. Pour into a well-oiled loaf pan or well-seasoned cast-iron skillet.

Bake at 350 degrees for about 30 minutes in a small skillet or 1 hour in a loaf pan. The top should spring back when lightly touched.

Variations: Add a drained small can of chopped green chiles; 1 cup shredded mild or sharp Cheddar cheese; 1 cup cooked and drained whole corn kernels; 1 cup creamed white corn (add 1/4 to 1/2 cup more cornmeal if the creamed corn contains a lot of liquid); or 1/2 cup well-drained cooked and crumbled bacon.

Makes 1 loaf

An easy way to make a lot of corn bread for a crowd or for the holiday dressing is to bake it in a 9x9-inch brownie pan and then cut it into squares. For corn bread dressing, make it a little drier than for eating out of hand, and crumble it into the bowl of cooked celery, onions, and poultry seasoning; moisten it with good chicken broth or gravy. Season it a lot with salt, pepper, and more poultry seasoning. It also makes a wonderful base for squash croquettes. Cook and thoroughly drain the squash, mash it, and add it to the dressing. You need about 3 times more squash than corn bread to make croquettes. Pat into squares or pyramids, and then roll in a beaten egg and then bread or cracker crumbs. Fry in about 1 inch of light vegetable oil until they are golden brown and cooked through.

Blue Cornmeal Quick Bread

Blue cornmeal is not as hard to find these days, with all the Tex-Mex interests in food and the easy availability of esoteric products, as it used to be. It gives a very decided texture to the quick bread, and the taste is usually a lot more "corny" than yellow cornmeal. You can substitute yellow or white cornmeal should you not be able to track down the blue, and the corn bread will still be good, but different.

2 cups blue cornmeal
2 tablespoons salt
1 tablespoon (scant) baking powder
2 eggs, beaten
1 cup (2 sticks) unsalted butter, melted
2 cups sour cream
2 cups white or blue corn, cooked and drained
8 ounces shredded sharp Cheddar cheese
1 small can green chiles, drained and chopped

Place paper muffin liners in muffin cups, and brush them lightly with oil. Combine the cornmeal, salt, and baking powder in a mixer bowl. Add the eggs, butter, sour cream, and corn. Mix well, but do not overmix. Fold in the cheese and green chiles.

Fill the prepared muffin cups a bit more than 2/3 full. Bake at 375 degrees for 20 to 25 minutes or until the center muffin tests done.

Makes about 14 muffins or 2 loaves

Corn Bubble Bread

This is one of my favorite breads from a very old magazine clipping that I have schlepped around for more than 20 years. The bubble bread looks delightfully homemade, especially with casual breakfast, brunch, or supper foods.

5 cups sifted all-purpose flour
2 cups cornmeal
2 tablespoons sugar
2 tablespoons yeast
1 tablespoon salt
2 cups milk
1/4 cup water
3 tablespoons unsalted butter, melted, or 3 tablespoons vegetable oil
1/2 cup (1 stick) unsalted butter, melted

Combine 2 cups of the flour, the cornmeal, sugar, yeast, and salt in a large mixer bowl. Beat with the paddle attachment until mixed.

Heat the milk, water, and 3 tablespoons melted butter in a saucepan until lukewarm. Pour into the flour mixture. Beat at low speed for several minutes or until the mixture is foamy. Change to the dough hook. With the mixer running at low speed, add 1/2 cup flour at a time, scraping the side of the bowl occasionally. Beat until the mixture begins to pull away from the side of the bowl. Knead at medium speed for 8 to 10 minutes or until the mixture is glossy and does not stick to the side of the bowl. It should be barely sticky to the touch. Let rise, covered, with a warm damp cloth, for about 1 hour or until doubled in bulk.

Punch down the dough. Roll the dough into a long fat roll. Cut into thirty-six 2-inch sections. Shape each section into a ball, and dip into the 1/2 cup melted butter. Arrange half the balls in a well-oiled 10-inch tube pan. (The balls should only touch lightly; rising will push them together.) Place the remaining balls in the pan. Let rise, covered, for about 1 hour or until doubled in bulk.

Bake at 375 degrees for 50 to 60 minutes or until the bread is golden brown and sounds hollow when tapped on the bottom. Remove from the pan, and place on a wire rack to cool. Brush with any remaining butter.

Makes 1 loaf

Professional bakeries hardly ever bother with these pretty breads, because they are a little labor-intensive compared to most loaf breads. I find they make wonderful quick-and-easy gifts for any holiday, wrapped in pretty plastic wrap and tied simply with plain twine or dressed up in an organza ribbon. Each bubble is pulled off one-by-one to be eaten.

Hush Puppies

Ben Bradley, my nephew, is as cute and sweet a young man as you will ever meet. He's just like his mother, my younger sister, Molly. When Ben was about four years old, his favorite place to eat was a fast-food fish-and-chips place. When it was his turn to order, he would count on his little fingers the things he wanted: "I want 2 shrimps, 1 fishes, 1 Tarsus sauce, and 3 dog balls." I have never made or served hush puppies without wanting to call Ben. He's grown and busy now, and, besides that, he's heard that family story so many times, he probably doesn't think it's funny anymore. I'm putting it here, so we will always remember it.

2 cups self-rising cornmeal mix
3 tablespoons self-rising flour
1 small onion, chopped
1^1/$_3$ cups buttermilk
1 egg, beaten
1 tablespoon Tabasco sauce
1 cup (or more) flavorless vegetable oil

Combine the cornmeal mix, flour, and onion in a large bowl. Combine the buttermilk, egg, and Tabasco sauce in a medium bowl, and mix well. Add the buttermilk mixture to the flour mixture. Mix with a fork until combined; do not overmix.

Bring 4 inches vegetable oil to a boil in a small heavy saucepan. Add small balls of dough to the saucepan 3 or 4 at a time; do not crowd the saucepan. Fry until golden brown, turning once. Remove and drain.

Add more oil to the saucepan if needed. If the oil is very hot when you add the balls of dough, the hush puppies will not absorb much of the oil at all, which is what you want. If the oil gets too hot, it will smoke. Let it cool, discard it, and start it again.

Makes about 18 small hush puppies

Oil temperature is very important when frying things, whether pan-frying or deep-frying. Peanut oil has the highest smoke point (burning temperature), but it also adds a noticeable but not unpleasant flavor. Also, some people are dangerously allergic to peanuts, so know your audience.

After each batch is removed from the oil, you can then add more oil and bring it back to the high temperature necessary. Do not add more oil during cooking, or it will lower the temperature of all the oil and the hush puppies (or whatever) will be too oily to eat.

Drain all fried foods well on paper towels. If I have a lot of fish to fry, I find it more economical to line my workspace with old newspapers, and then top the newspapers with clean paper towels. Then I just change the paper towels every now and then, because newspapers are so absorbent they don't have to be changed. It's a good way to catch up with the headlines, or the gossip column, or Dave Barry, and especially the food section, while you are just standing there frying.

Fiery Corn Muffins

"Fiery" foods are not my favorite foods, but sometimes they are necessary to bring out all the other flavors with which you may find yourself dealing. This especially applies to chiles and the like. It amazes me when I see my friends who are cake bakers, like Rose Berenbaum, my friend and teacher from years ago, eat the hottest of hot peppers and not even break a sweat. Rose is the best baker I have ever known. She is meticulous, exacting, and approaches baking as the scientist that she really is. Her baking results are proof positive of how important science (and love and understanding) are in work itself. I would love to be that exacting, I think. Actually, I am more like my friend Toby, whom I quote at the beginning of this chapter. Rose would consider these muffins bland, but this is about as far as I can go into the pepper scene. If you are like Rose, have at it. I'm sure you already know what to do to jazz them up. If you don't, there are many wonderful books on hot and spicy foods these days.

1 egg, beaten
1¹/₂ cups milk, low-fat milk, or nonfat milk
¹/₄ cup vegetable oil
2 cups self-rising cornmeal mix
2 teaspoons sugar
2 teaspoons crushed red pepper flakes
2 teaspoons dried dill

Mix the egg, milk, and vegetable oil in a large bowl. Add the cornmeal mix, sugar, red pepper flakes, and dill, stirring just until mixed. Pour into well-oiled muffin cups. Bake at 400 degrees for 15 to 20 minutes or until a wooden pick inserted near the center of the middle muffin comes out clean. Let stand for 10 minutes before serving.

Note: You can use paper liners in the muffin cups if you like, but spray them with nonstick cooking spray as well.

Makes 12 large or 24 small muffins

If you are making small muffins, be sure all your batter is well mixed or, sure enough, someone who hates peppery foods (like me) will get all the peppers in that one tiny muffin. Over-mixing muffins or any quick breads tends to make them tough, so you must mix everything together without getting too carried away.

These peppery muffins make wonderful tea or cocktail sandwiches. Split them in half, spread with a little melted unsalted butter, and fill with slivers of honey-cured ham or smoked turkey. They are rather fussy to do, especially the small ones, and they will separate into tops and bottoms and fillings if you don't press them together as you fill them. We used to do them by the hundreds (literally) for large cocktail parties, and we used frilled cocktail picks to hold them together in the serving baskets. Gwen Henry, our most patient and exacting cook and our catering director at the restaurant, was always in charge of these fiddle-y things. Her love and patience are what made them taste so good and hold together so well.

Mustard-y Corn Muffins

These muffins have just enough zing for folks like me, who really don't like hot, peppery foods. I especially like to pair these muffins with any of the casseroles in Chapter 1 that have ham, sausage, or chicken in them. A salad or some kind of fresh fruit or green vegetable accompaniment would give you the much-needed texture in your menu.

These muffins, large or small, are also wonderful carriers for ham, smoked turkey, or even chicken salad "sandwiches." Split the muffins, brush them with melted unsalted butter (or low-fat or nonfat butter substitute), add the meat filling, and press them together slightly. With ham slivers, I like to use guava jelly instead of the unsalted butter. It makes a wonderful combination of flavors. A crunchy vegetable salad, such as broccoli, would add texture.

3 tablespoons olive oil
2 green onions, finely chopped, with some of the
  green included
2 ribs celery, very finely chopped
2 cups plain cornmeal (white, if available)
1 cup all-purpose flour
1/4 cup sugar
1 teaspoon baking soda
2 teaspoons baking powder
2 teaspoons salt
2 cups buttermilk
3 tablespoons Dijon mustard
1/2 cup olive oil
1 cup shredded Cheddar cheese

Heat 3 tablespoons olive oil in a small skillet. Add the green onions and celery, and sauté until wilted. Mix the cornmeal, flour, sugar, baking soda, baking powder, and salt in a large bowl. Add the celery mixture, and mix well. Mix the buttermilk, Dijon mustard, and 1/2 cup olive oil in a small bowl. Add the buttermilk mixture and the cheese to the flour mixture, and mix well. Spoon or ladle into oiled muffin cups. Bake at 375 degrees for 30 minutes or until a wooden pick inserted near the center of the middle muffin comes out clean.

Note: You can use paper liners in the muffin cups if you like, but spray them with nonstick cooking spray as well.

Makes 12 large muffins

Whether desserts are "lowly" or "grand" usually depends on what kind of a baker you are. Some of the wonderful people who tested these recipes for me would classify any baking as "grand." Others who bake frequently found the "grand" recipes to be no challenge at all. The occasion is what is lowly or grand. "Ordinary days" are the 360 days of the year when there are no real holidays, no birthdays, just everyday-ness.

Those are the days that we need encouragement, support, and someone who cares. Whether it is a plate of biscuits, a couple of everyday muffins, or a grand layer cake does not really matter. What matters is that we took some time to remember someone, and that especially includes those in our families.

You have no idea what it means to someone who has been in the food business of some sort for almost thirty years now to have someone bake me a loaf cake or a plate of cookies or a pan of corn bread. Years ago, a young friend of mine, Nita Barnes, used to bring me wonderful baked goodies all the time. Once, she even baked me a birthday cake. Her sister, Peggy Townes, brought me love gifts, too. These were some of the best gifts I have ever received. There was so much love and un-self-consciousness in these young women's gifts that I will always treasure the memories of them. The cakes, cookies, brownies, breads (especially the banana breads, which I never found time to bake myself) were absolutely some of the best I have ever tasted. Good chefs always say that if there is no love in the kitchen, there is no good product on the plate.

These two sisters certainly give love away, and it becomes the very best part of them. The important thing to remember is that an ordinary day can always be transformed into a grand one, with their kind of thoughtfulness and a little bit (well, maybe a lot) of effort.

Baking
Desserts
for Occasions
Lowly & Grand

Contents

Miniature Chocolate Bundt Cakes

Little cakes are a passion of mine, and it is a good thing that they are, because they can be a real nuisance to make. These are quite easy. They are made in little bundt cake pans (see pages 170–171 under Sources) that are wonderful for tiny pumpkin cakes for Halloween and Thanksgiving. Here, they are in chocolate, with a snow-white icing drizzled down one or two sides of the creases of the finished cake. There is something special about having my own little cake all to myself. I like to fill them with fresh fruit, especially strawberries or cherries on these chocolate cakes, or a wonderful custard on an apple cake.

Almost any cake recipe will work in small pans as long as you size any chopped fruit, nuts, or chips to scale. On some of the pretty little two-inch square cake pans, one or two large chocolate chips would not leave much room for batter and just would not work. Use your imagination with small cakes, and allot yourself plenty of time and patience. It really is worth it.

1$^1/_2$ cups all-purpose flour	1$^3/_4$ cups sugar
1 cup baking cocoa	3 eggs
1$^1/_2$ teaspoons baking powder	1 tablespoon vanilla extract
$^1/_2$ teaspoon baking soda	2 cups confectioners' sugar
1 teaspoon salt	2 to 3 tablespoons heavy cream
1 cup (2 sticks) unsalted butter, softened	

Sift the flour, baking cocoa, baking powder, baking soda, and salt together, and set aside. Cream the butter and sugar in a mixer bowl until light and fluffy. Add the eggs one at a time, beating well after each addition. Add the vanilla, and mix well. Add the flour mixture to the creamed mixture gradually, beating at low speed just until mixed; do not overbeat. Spoon into 6 lightly oiled miniature bundt pans.

Bake at 350 degrees for 20 to 25 minutes or until a wooden pick inserted near the center comes out clean. Cool in the pans for 10 minutes. Remove to a wire rack to cool completely.

For the glaze, beat the confectioners' sugar and cream in a bowl with a fork until very thick. Let stand at least 15 minutes before using.

Drizzle the glaze down 1 or 2 of the crevices in the cakes, but don't totally obscure the pretty shapes of the cakes.

Makes 6 miniature cakes

The Real Red Velvet Cake
(Chocolate Beet Cake)

For 1 cup grated
beets, you will
probably need two
fresh beets about the
size of baseballs (not
softballs!). Scrub the
beets clean, but do not
peel them. Wrap each
beet tightly in foil, and
place them on a
baking sheet.

Bake at 375 degrees
for about 15 to 20
minutes or until they
can be penetrated by a
sharp knife inserted
near the center. Be
careful in opening the
foil to test for
doneness—they get
very hot. Remove to a
wire rack to cool.

When the beets are
cool to the touch, slip
the peel and roots off.
Grate as you would
carrots for a carrot
cake. Beets stain, so
wash your hands
immediately with
dishwashing
detergent.

2 cups cake flour
1/3 cup baking cocoa
1 teaspoon salt
2 teaspoons baking powder
1/2 cup corn oil
1 cup sugar
3 eggs
1/4 cup strawberry jam
2 teaspoons vanilla extract
1 cup grated cooked fresh beets
Grated zest of 1 medium orange
1 cup (6 ounces) semisweet chocolate chips

Lightly oil two 8-inch round cake pans. Line with waxed paper. Sift the flour, baking cocoa, salt, and baking powder together, and set aside.

Combine the corn oil and sugar in a large bowl, and mix well. Add the eggs one at a time, beating well after each addition. Mix the jam and vanilla in a small bowl. Add the flour mixture and jam alternately to the sugar mixture, beating well but quickly at low speed after each addition and scraping the side of the bowl occasionally. Add the beets and orange peel, and mix well. Stir in the chocolate chips.

Spoon the batter into the prepared cake pans. Tap each pan on a hard surface to remove any air bubbles.

Bake at 350 degrees for 25 to 30 minutes or until a wooden pick inserted near the center comes out clean. Let cool in the pans for 10 minutes. Remove to a wire rack to cool completely. Peel off the waxed paper. Spread your favorite cream cheese icing or Seven-Minute Marshmallow Icing (page 105) between the layers and over the top and side of the cooled cake.

Serves 12

Before you faint and fall over about beets in a cake, think about the first time someone told you about a carrot cake. You probably did not bat an eye. Beets, carrots, tomatoes, and many other vegetables are very high in sugar. A friend of mine from college days lived on a sugar plantation in Brusley, Louisiana, and even though they used sugar cane for their sugar, they were well aware of how important a product beets are for sugar. My grandfather was in the soft drink business here in Birmingham during the Second World War, when sugar was rationed. Our family grew up with a real interest in sugar production worldwide.

Like carrots, beets do wonderful things in baking. They not only add the obvious sugar, but their woodiness in texture adds moistness to the batter, too. Both vegetables add beautiful, natural color to the batter. The deep red beets add a deep burgundy color to the chocolate batter, and you already know about carrots in a spice cake and what a show they put on.

The chemists' next question could be about onions, because they are very high in sugar, too. I am going to leave that to you in cakes, but onions add magic to savory tarts and frittatas. Beets are a whole lot prettier and safer in a cake than a whole bottle of red food coloring. As my sister, Virginia, editorializes on some of her recipes to no one in particular (except herself), "Yuck. Nasty." And my favorite one: "Where did this come from? Who knows?"

Orange Marmalade Cake
(Fruits Cakes One)

This is a very old recipe from Stella Lockwood, our next-door neighbor in my old Forrest Park neighborhood here in Birmingham. I wrote quite a lot about her in my first book, Remembrances of Things Passed, *and I sent her one of the first copies of the book. She wrote me the cutest return letter, thanking me for recording all our sweet remembrances from those faraway days. She was in a nursing home in Jacksonville, Florida, and she died the next summer. I miss her every day.*

Stella was one of the few people in this world I liked calling me "Bon." She died in the heat of that summer in Jacksonville. The funeral was here in Birmingham, and Mother and my sister, Molly, went. Bill and I were in Italy that summer, and we did not get home until the end of September. Her son, Jack Lockwood, had been like a brother to me growing up, but I had not seen him in ten years, either.

Every now and then, I go by myself out to Elmwood Cemetery, although I know she is not really there, either, but I think she would have liked the idea of my going out there and leaving flowers. When I was little, I used to pull her roses off by their beautiful heads and take them to her with those beautiful flowers all squashed up in my hands. She never, ever fussed at me; in fact, she seemed genuinely glad to get them from me. I take long-stemmed roses now.

4^{1}/$_{4}$ cups cake flour or all-purpose flour, sifted
2 teaspoons salt
1^{1}/$_{2}$ teaspoons baking soda
1 (5-ounce) can evaporated milk
^{1}/$_{2}$ cup fresh orange juice
2 teaspoons vanilla extract
1 cup (2 sticks) unsalted butter, softened

1 cup sugar
3 eggs
1^{1}/$_{2}$ cups orange marmalade
Grated zest of 1 large orange
1 cup orange marmalade
Juice of 1 small lemon
2 teaspoons vanilla extract
Seven-Minute Marshmallow Icing (page 105)

Sift the flour, salt, and baking soda together; set aside. Mix the evaporated milk, orange juice, and 2 teaspoons vanilla in a bowl; set aside.

Cream the butter and sugar in a mixer bowl until light and fluffy. Add the eggs one at a time, beating well after each addition. Add 1^{1}/$_{2}$ cups orange marmalade and the orange zest, and mix well. Add the flour mixture and orange juice mixture alternately, mixing after each addition. Beat just until mixed, no longer than 5 minutes.

Spoon into 2 lightly oiled 8-inch round cake pans. Bake at 350 degrees for 25 to 30 minutes or until the layers test done. Remove from the oven. Let cool in the pans for 10 minutes. Remove to a wire rack to cool completely.

Mix 1 cup orange marmalade, the lemon juice, and 2 teaspoons vanilla in a bowl. Spread between the cake layers. Spread Seven-Minute Marshmallow Icing over the top and side of the cake. If desired, sprinkle with additional orange zest or pool an additional ^{1}/$_{4}$ cup marmalade in the center of the cake.

Serves 12

Seven-Minute Marshmallow Icing

1$^1/_2$ cups sugar
$^1/_4$ cup water
$^1/_4$ teaspoon cream of tartar
2 teaspoons salt
$^1/_2$ cup (about 4) egg whites
2 teaspoons vanilla extract
1 cup marshmallow creme

Beat the sugar, water, cream of tartar, and egg whites for 1 minute in the top of a double boiler with a handheld electric mixer. Set over boiling water, and beat for about 6 minutes or until the mixture resembles marshmallow creme and there is no trace of the sugar. Do not beat longer than a total of 7 or 8 minutes. Remove from the heat. Fold in the vanilla and marshmallow creme.

Makes about 2 cups

People have repeatedly questioned the title "Fruits Cakes Three," but what looks like a big typographical error is not. "Fruits Cakes" were cakes that we made and sold around the holiday season when I was in the bakery and catering business. Frankly, I love the genuine, authentic fruitcake, with all its candied fruits and nuts. Genuine fruitcakes are neither easy nor inexpensive to make. They take a lot of time, and then only to be the unworthy brunt of too many late-night TV comedians' jokes.

Here, then, is something different. Fruits Cakes are just that: three lovely cakes based on fruit. Apple Buttercake (that is, an apple buttercake, not a cake with apple butter); Orange Marmalade Cake; and Lemon Sweet Cake.

On pedestals of varied size and decorated with fresh fruit, these cakes are really lovely. No one would or could dare joke about them. I serve them with Russian Cream, a kind of blancmange that my sister, Virginia, sent me when I was a chef at a bed-and-breakfast in north Alabama.

For individual servings, I molded the Russian Cream (page 107) in lightly oiled muffin cups, then unmolded one on each dessert plate as an individual pudding. I then put a slice of Lemon Sweet Cake on the plate.

For a buffet, I placed the three cakes on their respective cake stands. Next to the cake stands, I served the Russian Cream in a large, footed glass compote.

Either way, these four desserts—the three cakes and the Russian Cream—are lovely and delicious.

Lemon Sweet Cake
(Fruits Cakes Two)

This is the second of the three "fruits cakes" that I like to use for holidays (even summer holidays) in the place of the time-consuming traditional dark Christmas fruitcake. The other two cakes, Apple Buttercake and Orange Marmalade Cake, are usually baked in different shapes from this cake.

Apple Buttercake is baked in a rectangular pan and is cut into thick squares, small rectangles, or even into small triangles. I serve them on a tray or in a lined flat cheese basket. Orange Marmalade Cake is a traditional round layer cake with its snowy white fluffy icing.

The Lemon Sweet Cake is really a rather "mock" pound cake, and it is baked in a loaf pan, then glazed. The Russian Cream in its lovely glass pedestal bowl is pure snow white. With it placed on a buffet, with all the cakes decorated with fresh strawberries, oranges, grapes, or fresh mint, you have a beautiful and luscious dessert table.

All of these Fruits Cakes Three (see page 105) can be prepared ahead. The Russian Cream can be done one day ahead, covered with plastic wrap, and refrigerated. The cakes can stay at room temperature for several days. I cover my cakes on their serving platter with an inverted large bowl. The bowls I use for the dome cakes are usually perfect "covers" since they are at least eight inches in diameter. They fit right over the tallest of these cakes, the Orange Marmalade.

1 1/2 cups all-purpose flour	3/4 cup (1 1/2 sticks) unsalted butter, softened
2 teaspoons salt	
1 1/2 teaspoons baking powder	1 1/4 cups sugar
Grated zest of 1 large lemon (about 1 tablespoon)	4 large eggs
	Lemon Glaze (sidebar, page 107)
1/2 cup whipping cream	Fresh mint, or any pretty grapes
1 tablespoon vanilla extract	or berries, for garnish

Mix the flour, salt, baking powder, and lemon zest in a bowl. Mix the whipping cream and vanilla in a bowl. Cream the butter and sugar in a mixer bowl for 10 minutes or until blended. Add the eggs one at a time, beating well after each addition. Add the flour and cream mixture alternately, mixing well after each addition; do not overbeat.

Spoon into a lightly oiled waxed paper-lined 4x8-inch loaf pan. Bang the pan on a hard surface to remove any air bubbles. Bake at 350 degrees for about 45 to 60 minutes or until a wooden pick inserted near the center comes out clean. (This is a dense cake, and it may take as long as 1 1/4 hours to bake. Begin testing it at 45 minutes.)

Let cool in the pan on a wire rack for about 10 minutes or until it pulls away from the side of the pan. Remove to a wire rack, and remove the waxed paper. Gently poke very small holes in the cake for the glaze to run through. Pour the Lemon Glaze over the cake over a platter, and reuse any dripped glaze. Repeat with a second layer of glaze if needed. Garnish with fresh mint or any pretty grapes or berries.

Makes 12 servings

Russian Cream

3 tablespoons unflavored gelatin
3/4 cup liqueur or orange juice
   (see Note)
1 1/2 cups boiling water
1 1/2 cups sugar
1 teaspoon salt

3 cups whipping cream
1 tablespoon vanilla extract
3 cups sour cream
Berries, fresh mint, and sliced
   oranges or whole strawberries

Dampen a mold and line with plastic wrap; set aside. (You can use lightly oiled individual custard cups or muffin cups instead; they make a lovely shape.)

Sprinkle the gelatin over the liqueur in a small saucepan. Let stand until the gelatin has softened. Cook over low heat until the gelatin is dissolved, stirring constantly until the mixture is clear. Be careful not to flame the liqueur, which is high in alcohol.

Pour the boiling water into a bowl. Add the gelatin mixture, stirring until clear. Add the sugar, stirring until dissolved. Add the salt, and mix well. Stir in the whipping cream, vanilla, and sour cream. Whisk until the mixture is blended and smooth.

Pour into the prepared mold. Chill in the refrigerator for several hours, preferably overnight. Unmold onto a lightly oiled platter so that you can move the cream around on the platter. Decorate with berries, mint, and sliced oranges or whole strawberries.

This is a delicious accompaniment to any of Fruits Cakes Three. This recipe can be halved.

Note: You can use a liqueur like Grand Marnier, an apricot liqueur, or plain orange juice, or a combination of any or all of them.

Makes about 1 quart (15 servings)

For the Lemon Glaze, combine the juice of 1 large lemon, 2 1/2 cups confectioners' sugar, and 1 teaspoon vanilla extract in a bowl. Mix with a fork until a smooth paste forms. Add more confectioners' sugar a little at a time if needed. Let stand for at least 20 minutes before using.

Makes about 2 1/2 cups

Apple Buttercake
(Fruits Cakes Three)

When we were in the bakery and restaurant business, we made so many of these cakes the first two years we were in business that we would put on the daily order sheets in the kitchen: "Another ABC cake; this makes 8 today (so far)." Sharon Campbell, our real chef, finally took the recipe, multiplied it by ten, baked it in a sheet pan, poured the icing over the top, and then cut the whole thing into two even sections. She then stacked the layers. It worked very nicely, because you got the same thickness of a cake, but with the added filling as well as the topping. We could cut the layered cake into any square or rectangular design we wanted. Now that I am back to smaller ovens, smaller muscles, and smaller ways of thinking, I bake the ABC cake in a 9x13-inch pan and serve it in squares like brownies. Cinnamon Ice Cream (at left) is delicious with it.

To make Cinnamon Ice Cream, mix 1 tablespoon ground cinnamon with a pinch of fresh nutmeg. Blend thoroughly into 1 quart of very good softened French vanilla ice cream.

1$1/2$ cups vegetable oil
2 cups sugar
2 eggs, beaten
1 tablespoon vanilla extract
2$1/2$ cups all-purpose flour
2 teaspoons salt
2 teaspoons baking powder
1 teaspoon baking soda
1$1/2$ cups chopped pecans
3 cups chopped peeled Gala or
   other hard apples
Butter Icing (below)

Beat the vegetable oil, sugar, eggs, and vanilla in a mixer bowl until mixed well. Mix the flour, salt, baking powder, baking soda, and pecans in a bowl. Add to the egg mixture, and beat quickly but thoroughly. Stir in the apples. Spoon into a well-oiled and waxed paper-lined 9x13-inch cake pan. Bake at 350 degrees for 45 to 50 minutes or until a wooden pick inserted near the center comes out clean. Let stand until just warm. Invert onto a lightly oiled serving platter, and remove the waxed paper. Punch small holes at regular intervals in the cake (so the icing can seep into the cake). Spoon the Butter Icing over the top of the cake.

Makes 12 servings

Butter Icing

1$1/2$ cups sugar
1 (5-ounce) can evaporated milk
1 cup chopped pecans
$1/4$ cup bourbon
$1/2$ cup (1 stick) unsalted butter

Bring the sugar, evaporated milk, pecans, bourbon, and butter to a boil in a saucepan, stirring constantly. Let cool to room temperature.

Makes about 2$1/2$ cups

Coconut Pound Cake

Years ago, someone brought a crunchy coconut pound cake to a Bible study I was in, and I almost missed Jane Anderson's wonderful lesson that day for trying to find out who brought the cake. Just to keep me attentive, my group leader stopped the discussion, asked the question, and Marilyn Harland thus helped restore my spirituality by promising me this recipe.

Actually, I think it was a spiritual quest in its own right. You will think so, too, if you like coconut and pound cake as much as I do. If not, you can bake the very simple pound cake and substitute any other flavoring that you like, rather than coconut. Lemon, plain vanilla with a little dark rum, bourbon, or orange in the glaze will give you a great pound cake by any other name.

3 cups cake flour, sifted
1/2 teaspoon baking powder
1 teaspoon salt
1 cup (2 sticks) unsalted butter, softened
1/2 cup vegetable shortening
3 cups sugar
5 eggs
1 1/4 cups milk

2 teaspoons vanilla extract
2 teaspoons coconut flavoring, almond flavoring, grated lemon zest, or grated orange zest
2 cups sugar
1/2 cup water
2 teaspoons coconut flavoring, almond flavoring, grated lemon zest, or grated orange zest

Sift the flour, baking powder, and salt together; set aside. Cream the butter, shortening, and 3 cups sugar in a mixer bowl for at least 10 minutes. (You cannot over-cream it. There should be no graininess from the sugar at the end of the creaming.) Add the eggs one at a time, beating well after each addition. Add the flour mixture and milk alternately, beating at medium speed after each addition; do not overbeat once the flour has been added. Stir in the vanilla and 2 teaspoons flavoring.

Spoon the batter into a well-oiled and floured tube pan. Bake at 325 degrees for about 1 1/2 hours or until a cake tester inserted near the center comes out clean. Remove from the oven, and let cool in the pan on a wire rack for 10 minutes. Remove to a wire rack with a tray underneath. Punch small holes at regular intervals in the top of the cake.

For the glaze, bring 2 cups sugar and the water to a boil in a saucepan, stirring constantly until the sugar is dissolved. Let cool to room temperature. Stir in 2 teaspoons flavoring. Ladle over the warm cake. Repeat the glazing 3 times. Let stand at room temperature to harden the glaze.

Serves 12

Upside-Down Gingerbread

Gingerbread is one of my favorite comfort foods. This recipe came from my sister in Nashville, who I think got it from a garden club gathering. She doesn't remember, either, but years ago, she did note on the tattered copy the date that she sent it to me: "summer, '67."

The original recipe apparently called for lard, which is another wonderful baking fat, but not even I can be that politically incorrect. Don't scoff at lard in pastry-making, though. It definitely makes the very best piecrusts. I bet you don't even know where to find it in the grocery store. I'll leave that little conundrum for your next scavenger hunt at the supermarket. I know you can hardly wait.

2$^1/_2$ cups all-purpose flour
1 teaspoon each baking powder,
   baking soda, salt, cinnamon,
   and ginger
1 cup each sugar and shortening
3 eggs
1 cup dark molasses
   (not blackstrap)

$^2/_3$ cup buttermilk
3 tablespoons unsalted butter,
   melted
2 cups packed dark brown sugar
4 cups drained crushed pineapple
Sweetened Whipped Cream
   (at left)

To make Sweetened Whipped Cream, beat 2 cups whipping cream, $^1/_2$ cup confectioners' sugar, 1 tablespoon vanilla extract, and $^1/_8$ teaspoon salt in a mixer bowl just until soft peaks begin to form (it should look like a custard, rather than a stiff icing). Sprinkle with ginger or nutmeg to taste.

Makes about 4 cups

Sift the flour, baking powder, baking soda, salt, cinnamon, and ginger together; set aside. Cream the sugar and shortening in a mixer bowl until light and fluffy. Add the eggs one at a time, beating at medium speed after each addition. After the last egg is beaten in, beat at high speed until well mixed, scraping the side of the bowl frequently. Beat in the molasses. Add the buttermilk, and beat at low speed until mixed. It will be quite liquid. Beat in the flour mixture gradually. Scrape the bowl frequently to incorporate all the dry ingredients. Check the bottom of the bowl frequently, and scrape the beaters as well. Do not overbeat from this point on. Stir with a large kitchen spoon, if necessary.

Mix the butter with the brown sugar, and combine with the pineapple in a bowl. Lightly oil a 10x13-inch baking pan, and line the pan with waxed paper. Oil the paper as well (to keep the pineapple mixture from sticking). Spoon the pineapple mixture into the prepared pan. Spoon the batter carefully over the pineapple. Gently tap the pan on a solid surface to force any air bubbles to the top.

Bake at 350 degrees for 45 to 50 minutes or until a wooden pick inserted near the center comes out clean. Cool in the pan for 10 minutes. Remove the cake to a lightly oiled serving platter. The pineapple will be on the top, the gingerbread on the bottom. Top the warm cake with Sweetened Whipped Cream.

Makes 12 servings

Cherry Cream Pie

A book of nothing but recipes using fresh cherries would suit me fine. I doubt, however, if I would get very far with such a book, because I love fresh crunchy cherries just as they come from the tree (or, for me here in the South, from the crate). However, Bette and Finley McRae, who share my passion for cherries, send me bags of them, and I buy them myself whenever I save up my money.

I preserve most of them in vodka, with lots of sugar and a vanilla bean or two. I then refrigerate them for months (see page 125). Obviously, I can only put so many in vodka, and, even with wild game, you don't use very many in a sauce. Therefore, I put together this Cherry Cream Pie, which I think does the whole wonderful world of cherries a great service. I think it could be absolutely guaranteed to make a fanatic out of you, too. Or, try the clafouti, or the . . .

1/2 cup packed dark brown sugar	1 cup sugar
4 cups fresh cherries, pitted, juice strained and reserved	1 tablespoon vanilla extract
	2 eggs, beaten
1 unbaked pie pastry, prepared from Betty Sims' Perfect Piecrust recipe (page 113)	2 teaspoons salt
	1 teaspoon freshly ground nutmeg
	1 cup sour cream
1/2 cup melted red currant jelly	2 tablespoons confectioners' sugar
16 ounces cream cheese, softened	1 teaspoon vanilla extract

Sprinkle the brown sugar over the cherries. Fit the pie pastry into a lightly oiled 9-inch tart pan or 4 individual tart pans. "Paint" the pastry with the melted jelly to seal the crusts during baking. Reserve the unused jelly for the cherries.

Beat the cream cheese, sugar, 1 tablespoon vanilla, the eggs, salt, and nutmeg in a mixer bowl until blended and smooth. Spoon into the pastry in the tart pan. Place on a baking sheet.

Bake at 350 degrees until a knife inserted near the center comes out clean (about 35 minutes for the large tart or 15 to 20 minutes for the smaller tarts). Remember that the pie will continue to bake after being removed from the oven, so do not allow it to dry out during baking.

Spoon the cherry mixture onto the cooled pie. Mix the reserved juice from the cherries with the reserved melted jelly. Brush liberally over the cherries to glaze them. Mix the sour cream, confectioners' sugar, and 1 teaspoon vanilla in a bowl. Top each serving with a dollop of the sour cream mixture.

Makes 1 open-face tart, or 4 individual tarts

Butterscotch Pie

This is one of those recipes from my sister in Nashville that dates back from the early '60s and has more notes around it than the original had ingredients. She baked for a women's club for a while, and this was one of their favorite pies. I have never found a pie-eater who didn't like it. You can use a graham cracker crust, but I like the salty taste of Betty Sims' Perfect Piecrust with this sweet caramel.

1 unbaked pie pastry, prepared from Betty Sims' Perfect Piecrust recipe
    (page 113)
1 cup packed dark brown sugar
1 teaspoon salt
1/4 cup all-purpose flour
2 cups milk
4 egg yolks, beaten
2 tablespoons unsalted butter, melted and cooled
2 teaspoons vanilla extract
Meringue Topping (page 113)

Fit the pie pastry into a pie plate. Bake at 375 degrees for 8 to 10 minutes or until lightly browned. Let stand to cool.

Combine the brown sugar, salt, and flour in a saucepan, and mix well. Whisk in the milk gradually. Cook over medium heat until the mixture is thickened and beginning to coat a spoon, stirring constantly.

Combine the egg yolks and melted butter in a bowl, and mix gently. Add a small amount of the hot milk mixture to the egg yolks, whisking constantly to keep from cooking the eggs. Once the egg yolks have blended with the milk, add the egg yolk mixture to the saucepan. Cook over medium heat for 1 to 2 minutes or until the mixture is thick enough to coat a spoon, stirring constantly. Stir in the vanilla.

If there are any lumps, strain the custard through a sieve into the baked crust. Let stand at room temperature for at least 1 hour.

Spoon the Meringue Topping over the pie, spreading the meringue all the way to the edge. Broil until the tips of the meringue are browned. Serve within 2 hours if possible. (If you must chill the pie, the meringue will shrink somewhat. It is better to add the meringue just before serving.)

Makes 1 pie

Betty Sims' Perfect Piecrust

2 cups all-purpose flour
1 teaspoon salt
3/4 cup (1 1/2 sticks) unsalted butter
3 tablespoons chilled vegetable shortening
1/4 cup (about) ice water

Combine the flour and salt in a food processor. Cut in the butter and shortening. Process for a few seconds until the mixture resembles coarse meal. Add the water 1 drop at a time, processing very briefly after each addition. (The entire process should take 20 to 30 seconds.) Wrap the dough in plastic wrap, and chill for at least 1 hour.

Makes two 9-inch pie pastries, or one double-crust pastry

Meringue Topping

1 cup egg whites (6 to 8)
1 teaspoon salt
1 teaspoon cream of tartar
1/2 cup (scant) superfine sugar
2 teaspoons vanilla extract

Beat the egg whites, salt, and cream of tartar at low speed in a mixer bowl just until foamy. Add the sugar 1 tablespoon at a time, beating at high speed until the sugar is incorporated. Beat at high speed for several minutes or until the egg whites resemble melted marshmallows. Stir in the vanilla quickly.

Makes 1 meringue

My Old Kentucky Pie

You can make a very decorative pie with any leftover dough. Cut the chilled dough into shapes, such as leaves, circles, or tiny hearts, and bake them separately on a lightly oiled foil-lined cookie sheet for just a few minutes, until browned.

Use a little of the wet ganache to stick the dough pieces around the edge of the baked pie. This way, the pieces are not baked on the pie, and therefore they do not burn around the edges. Another of my grandmother's "baking secrets." Do things separately, if necessary. All's fair in pie making, you know.

1/2 cup (1 stick) unsalted butter
1/2 cup sugar
2 cups ground pecans
1 cup sifted all-purpose flour
Grated zest of 1 small lemon
2 egg yolks
2 tablespoons Kentucky bourbon
3/4 cup packed dark brown sugar
4 eggs, beaten
6 tablespoons unsalted butter, melted and cooled
2/3 cup dark corn syrup
1/3 cup molasses (not blackstrap)
Grated zest of 1 small lemon
2 tablespoons Kentucky bourbon, or 1 tablespoon vanilla extract
2 teaspoons salt
Ganache Topping (sidebar, page 115)
Fresh mint leaves, for garnish

For the Pecan Piecrust, cream 1/2 cup butter and the sugar in a food processor. Add the pecans, flour, and lemon zest. Pulse on and off just until smooth. Mix the egg yolks and 2 tablespoons bourbon in a cup. Add to the flour mixture. Mix just until the dough forms a ball. Chill, wrapped in plastic wrap, for at least 1 hour.

Press the dough into a circle on a lightly floured surface, then quickly roll into a flat circle. Pat into a lightly oiled 9-inch pie plate. Chill for at least 1 hour.

For the filling, combine the brown sugar, eggs, and 6 tablespoons butter in a mixer bowl, and mix well. Add the corn syrup, molasses, lemon zest, 2 tablespoons bourbon, and the salt, and mix well.

Spoon the filling into the chilled pie shell. Bake at 350 degrees for 25 to 30 minutes or until a knife inserted near the center comes out clean. Let stand to cool. Pour the Ganache Topping over the pie while the topping is still pourable but not hot. Do not let the topping go down into the side of the pie, or the topping will make it difficult to get the slices out of the pie plate. Garnish with fresh mint leaves—a real Kentucky Derby touch!

Makes 1 pie

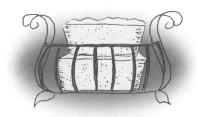

It's funny how things seem to come full circle. "Little Doc's" memorial service was held at the same beautiful church in which his oldest grandson had been married just a few years before. Well, okay, it was probably five years or more before.

As I sat there at the memorial service remembering Julie, the bride, and Sterling, the groom, leaving the church together to melodic triumphant hymns of joy, I thought that perhaps a memorial service can be, and should be, a kind of triumphant occasion. There is still a sense of immortality, of closing, and opening, and beginning again that pervades both occasions.

The last anthem sung at Dr. Coleman's memorial service was sung a cappella by a beautiful young woman, and there were no bells pealing, no applauding on this earth—just the echoes of that haunting solitary voice singing, "Weep no more, my lady . . . for the sun shines bright on my old Kentucky home, my old Kentucky home far away."

Dr. Coleman's daughter, Caroline, was my best friend growing up, and she would think nothing of facing down a herd of horses if necessary. There was little she couldn't do, actually, and we were both usually in big trouble because of it, too! Horses were always her heart, and they were a lot less apt to get us grounded. My oldest son, Charles (her godson), and his wife, Kris, and daughters Katherine and Anne just spent some time with Caroline in the horse country where she now lives. They and my other two grandchildren, Jack and Chloe, think this Grand Bonnie of theirs is one cool lady for having such a savvy, cool, snazzy childhood friend! This, then, is Caroline's pie . . . for a deeply sweet and beautiful person, and a flat-out bribe to have us all back again soon.

For the Ganache Topping, melt 8 ounces semisweet chocolate chips in a double boiler over hot water, stirring until smooth. Add 3/4 cup warmed whipping cream, stirring until smooth. If the chocolate seizes (clumps or hardens), add 1 tablespoon unsalted butter or tasteless vegetable oil and 1 tablespoon hot water, stirring constantly until smooth.

Makes about 2 cups

Fig Fudge Pie

The last time that I saw my best friend and college roommate from my New Orleans days, I found this recipe tucked inside her usual neat recipe notebooks. She died that same year, and I have never told anyone its history.

All that and so much else took place a long, long time ago, but it seems like yesterday that we were sitting in her beautiful kitchen that spring morning going over recipes, drinking the best iced coffee in the world, and eating honeydew melon. That had been our routine all through college and the decade or so following. We had even lived in New York together one year, and we spent many summer breakfasts at other places in that simple routine.

After she died, I did not go back to New Orleans as often as I had before. Her house and all in it has long since been sold, and no one cared about the recipes except the two of us, so, technically, this was my last present from her, except for her persona. That will never leave me.

2 cups fresh figs, or 1 cup dried figs
1/3 cup brandy or Cognac
1 unbaked pie pastry, prepared from Betty Sims' Perfect Piecrust recipe
  (page 113)
1 cup semisweet chocolate chips
1 cup (2 sticks) unsalted butter
6 eggs, beaten
2 cups sugar
1 teaspoon salt
1 teaspoon vanilla extract
2 tablespoons confectioners' sugar
1 tablespoon vanilla extract
1 cup whipped cream

Mince the figs, and soak them in the brandy for at least 1 hour (overnight if using dried figs). Fit the pie pastry into a pie plate.

Melt the chocolate chips and butter in a heatproof bowl in the microwave or over a double boiler. Add the eggs, sugar, salt, and 1 teaspoon vanilla. Whisk until mixed well. Stir in the soaked figs. Spoon into the pie pastry. Bake at 350 degrees for 50 to 60 minutes or until a knife inserted near the center comes out clean.

Fold the confectioners' sugar and 1 tablespoon vanilla into the whipped cream. Top each serving with the sweetened whipped cream.

Makes 1 pie

Creamy Rhubarb Pie

When we were growing up, we had rhubarb quite a lot. It keeps nicely over the winter, stewed and "put up" in Mason jars. Cooked, it made a wonderful winter dessert with boiled custard. As seasonal fruits began to disappear into year-round fruits, strawberries seemed to replace rhubarb in our pies and desserts. Rhubarb is too good to be left out. It is very high in vitamin C, and its tart flavor and wonderful texture add much to a pie or cobbler.

The leaves of rhubarb are not edible; in fact, they are quite toxic, but they are usually trimmed by the time the fleshy stems get to the produce counter. Because it is very acid, like most fruits, rhubarb does strange things in custards. In this recipe, marinate the rhubarb first, set it aside until time to make the custard (if you are doing them over a period of time), and then join them together just as you put them into the oven. You'll be glad you did. It won't hurt anything if you don't; it just does not bake as nicely.

5 cups fresh rhubarb
1 tablespoon vanilla extract
3 tablespoons dark brown sugar
1 unbaked pie pastry, prepared from Betty Sims' Perfect Piecrust recipe
  (page 113)
2 teaspoons strawberry, quince, or red currant jelly or jam, melted
2 cups heavy cream
1 cup sugar
2/3 cup all-purpose flour
1 teaspoon freshly grated nutmeg
2 eggs, beaten

Cut all the leaves away from the rhubarb. Cut the rhubarb into 1-inch chunks. Combine the vanilla and brown sugar in a bowl, and mix well. Add the rhubarb, and marinate until baking time.

Fit the pie pastry into a 9-inch pie plate. Brush the pastry with the melted jelly to seal the crust during baking.

For the custard, combine the cream, sugar, flour, nutmeg, and eggs in a saucepan, and mix well. Cook until thickened, whisking until all the flour has dissolved.

Combine the custard and the rhubarb mixture in a bowl, and mix gently. Spoon into the pie pastry. Bake at 350 degrees for 40 minutes or until a knife inserted near the center comes out clean.

Makes 1 pie

Walnut Apple Pie

For the whipped cream or sauce that sometimes goes over a pie or cobbler, I serve each guest with an individual little cream pitcher (if I don't have too many guests). In Birmingham years ago, a very popular restaurant group used to serve delicious individual apple pies with a wonderful "cream" over them. After the restaurant closed, people continually wrote Joellen O'Hara, The Birmingham News food editor, about obtaining the "secret sauce recipe." Finally, several employees from the then-defunct restaurant verified that it was nothing more than Eagle Brand sweetened condensed milk, right out of the can.

1 unbaked pie pastry, prepared from Betty Sims' Perfect Piecrust recipe (page 113)
4 or 5 firm apples, such as Galas, cut into chunks
1/2 cup packed dark brown sugar
2 teaspoons cinnamon
2 teaspoons freshly ground nutmeg
2 teaspoons cardamom
Grated zest of 1 small lemon
Juice of 1/2 small lemon
1 1/2 cups sour cream, low-fat sour cream, or nonfat sour cream
1 (14-ounce) can Eagle Brand sweetened condensed milk
1/4 cup frozen apple juice concentrate, thawed
2 eggs
2 teaspoons vanilla extract
2 tablespoons unsalted butter, melted
Streusel Topping (at left)

Fit the pie pastry into a pie plate. Bake at 350 degrees for 15 minutes or until lightly browned. Set aside.

Combine the apples and brown sugar in a bowl and mix gently. Add the cinnamon, nutmeg, cardamom, lemon zest, and lemon juice, and mix gently. Marinate at room temperature for at least 1 hour.

Beat the sour cream, condensed milk, apple juice concentrate, eggs, and vanilla in a mixer bowl until blended and smooth. Spoon into the partially baked pie shell. Bake at 350 degrees for 30 minutes or until set. Let cool slightly.

Heat the butter in a skillet. Add the apple mixture. Cook just until the apples are tender. Remove to a bowl.

Spread the apple mixture over the top of the pie. Spoon the Streusel Topping over the apples.

Serves 6 to 8

For the Streusel Topping, combine 1 cup dark brown sugar, 1/4 cup all-purpose flour, 2 teaspoons cinnamon, 1 cup melted unsalted butter, 2 teaspoons salt, and 1 cup chopped walnuts in a skillet. Cook over medium heat until the walnuts are lightly toasted and the flour has dissolved, stirring constantly.

Makes about 2 1/2 cups

I was the spokesperson for the blue label, low-fat Eagle Brand sweetened condensed milk when it came out in the 1990s. Nissa Rachlin, Tara Johnson, Veronica Petti, and I were "new best friends" for almost a year that year. The project ended in October when we filmed Christmas ads at my house here in Birmingham.

My neighbors thought I had lost my mind decorating for Christmas in October. We had to film inside and out in the hot Alabama sun. The campaign was a busy one and was certainly educational for all of us.

At one point, we had to dress Cathy Muir, the food stylist, in one of my outfits for the film, because the UPS man who showed up at the door refused to be in the video. (We were desperate!)

Gail Little, the general stylist, and Cathy and I look like real southern ladies in all the ads, not like the requisitioned chef, stylists, and general warm bodies that we really were. I love the videos to this day; everything just fell into place. Gail, always impeccable, even had a brand-new manicure. Cathy, who could wear a sack and still be beautiful, looked so good in my outfit that I myself never wore it again. Nissa really envied the dress I wore, and I should have given it to her right then, because it got covered with the perfect Sweet Traditions Truffles that Cathy had made and I never wore it again (the dress, that is). I have "worn" the truffles on lots of outfits since then.

"Eagle Brand low-fat sweetened condensed milk" was a phrase I could and did say in my sleep. Now Borden has also made a nonfat sweetened condensed milk, but I think Elsie represented them for that product. All three (regular, low-fat, and nonfat) are absolutely wonderful products, and they certainly brought me many wonderful co-workers, whom I remember with great fondness.

Clementine Tart

Clementines used to be an anomaly to most cooks. Now, however, they are found in almost all markets from Thanksgiving through spring. They are difficult to eat out of hand because they are so small, but they make wonderful pies. If you don't like to fool with the little clementines, this recipe works quite well if you juice fresh tangerines and use mandarin orange slices instead of the clementines.

3 cups all-purpose flour
1/2 cup sugar
1 teaspoon salt
1 egg
1 egg yolk
6 tablespoons unsalted butter,
    softened
1 to 2 tablespoons sugar

Grated zest and juice of
    6 clementines (about 1 cup juice)
6 egg yolks, beaten
1 egg, beaten
2 cups heavy cream
2 teaspoons salt
2 teaspoons vanilla extract
4 to 6 clementine sections

For the tart shell, combine the flour, 1/2 cup sugar, and 1 teaspoon salt in a bowl, and mix well. Add 1 egg and 1 egg yolk, and mix quickly. Add the butter. Knead the mixture with the heel of your hand for 1 or 2 turns, or just until the butter begins to be mashed into the dough. Pat the dough into a ball, and wrap it in plastic wrap. Refrigerate for at least 2 hours.

Roll the chilled dough into a circle on a lightly floured surface. Fit into one 9-inch fluted tart pan or four 6-inch tart pans. Prick the bottom of the dough, and sprinkle with 1 to 2 tablespoons sugar. Refrigerate the tart shell until baking time.

For the filling, combine the clementine zest, clementine juice, 6 egg yolks, 1 egg, the cream, and 2 teaspoons salt in a double boiler, and beat well. Cook over medium heat until the mixture begins to thicken. Stir in the vanilla.

Spoon the filling into the chilled pie shell. Place on a baking sheet. Bake at 350 degrees for about 10 to 20 minutes or until the filling is set. Chill until serving time.

Clean all the pith from the clementine sections. Dry the sections with a clean cloth. Arrange attractively over the pie filling.

Makes one 9-inch tart, or four 6-inch tarts

Lemon Shaker Tart

A "Lemon Shaker Tart" is not at all the same thing as lemon icebox pie. A "Shaker tart" is usually a lot more tart than our Southern standby, and it has no meringue or whipped cream topping.

3 cups all-purpose flour
1/2 cup sugar
1 teaspoon salt
1 egg
1 egg yolk
6 tablespoons unsalted butter, softened
Grated zest and juice of 4 large lemons (about 3/4 cup juice)

1 cup (2 sticks) unsalted butter, softened
1 cup sugar
5 large eggs, beaten
2 teaspoons vanilla extract
4 large lemons
1 cup sugar

For the tart shell, mix the flour, 1/2 cup sugar, and the salt in a large bowl. Add 1 egg and 1 egg yolk, and mix well Add the 6 tablespoons butter 1 tablespoon at a time, beating until the butter is almost completely incorporated. Place the dough on a lightly floured surface. With the heel of your hand, spread the dough quickly several times as though to knead it. When it seems to come together, pat it into a ball. Wrap in plastic wrap; chill in the refrigerator for at least 2 hours. Roll out the dough, and fit it into a 9-inch fluted tart pan. Prick the bottom of the dough with a fork. Sprinkle with sugar to taste.

For the filling, combine the lemon zest and lemon juice in a nonreactive double boiler. Add 1 cup butter and 1 cup sugar, and beat well. Add 5 eggs. Cook over medium heat until the custard begins to thicken, whisking constantly. Remove from the heat, and stir in the vanilla. Spoon the filling into the pie shell. Bake at 350 degrees for 20 to 30 minutes or until the filling is set. Let cool completely. Cut 4 lemons into 1/8- to 1/4-inch slices. Place on a lightly oiled foil-lined baking sheet. Sprinkle sugar over the slices, almost completely covering each slice. Bake at 250 to 275 degrees for 1 hour or until both sides of the lemons are hard and beginning to dry out. Turn the slices once during baking, but be careful not to burn yourself on the hot sugar. Arrange attractively over the top of the pie.

Makes one 9-inch tart, or several smaller tarts

In the southern United States, a "lemon pie" is a lemon icebox pie, made with Eagle Brand sweetened condensed milk. I know this because I have lived in the South most of my life (and also because I was the spokesperson for Eagle Brand's low-fat sweetened condensed milk). We pitched the new blue-label product mostly in the midwest and some on the West Coast, because it is such a strong product in the South. With my Southern accent, I think I represented the product right well. All three Eagle Brand products (regular, low-fat, and nonfat) are wonderful, so the campaign was easy for me.

Blueberry Cobbler

Traditionally, this is probably not a cobbler, in that it is sort of a reversed version of what we usually know as cobblers. I like this kind of inverted pudding and pie, because the dough part tends to get all sopped up with juice, which is the part my family loves best. There are all sorts of old-fashioned names for these different fruit pies, like buckle, grunt, and, if topped with oatmeal, crisps. I call them all cobblers. A rose by any other name . . .

Years ago, Gwen Henry, Betty Sims, and I went to Martha Stewart's lovely home in Westport, Connecticut, for a catering seminar. Martha is a very generous and gracious hostess, as you can well imagine. Everything she does is true and real and very, very good. "A good thing" is an enormous understatement, to say the least.

One of the warnings she gave us about using fresh blueberries (such as she had growing in abundance in that magnificent garden of hers) had to do with a very important political figure for whom Martha had catered, using Martha's scrumptious baby blueberries for a delectable blueberry tart. Oddly enough, the great dignitary had worn all blue that day—hat, shoes, suit—and when she arose to speak, her blueberry-dyed teeth fully complemented the entire outfit! I love that story.

5 cups fresh blueberries
1/2 cup packed brown sugar
Grated zest of 1 small lemon
Juice of 1/2 small lemon (about 2 tablespoons)
1 tablespoon vanilla extract
1/2 cup (1 stick) unsalted butter, melted
2 cups all-purpose flour
2 cups sugar
1 teaspoon salt
2 1/2 teaspoons baking powder
1 1/2 cups milk
1 cup whipping cream (optional)
2 tablespoons confectioners' sugar (optional)
1 tablespoon vanilla extract (optional)

Combine the blueberries, brown sugar, lemon zest, lemon juice, and 1 tablespoon vanilla in a bowl, and mix well. Set aside.

Pour the melted butter into a 9x9-inch baking pan. Combine the flour, sugar, salt, and baking powder in a bowl, and mix well. Stir in the milk. Spoon the mixture into the baking pan. Spread the blueberry mixture over the batter, spreading all the way into the corners.

Bake at 375 degrees for 30 to 45 minutes or until the dough tests done with a fork. Beat the whipping cream, confectioners' sugar, and 1 tablespoon vanilla in a mixer bowl until thickened. Serve with the cobbler.

You can serve this cobbler with lemon-flavored yogurt instead of the sweetened whipped cream, if you prefer.

Serves 6 to 8

Peach Cobbler

Cobblers are ideal summer foods. They can be baked ahead and reheated, and they become even better from the process. Many a night, hunger has been staved off with a bowl or two of the cobbler, cold, right out of the refrigerator. For a recalcitrant breakfast eater, or even for a person who needs to eat but cannot because of some untoward health reasons, cobblers are real comforts.

8 medium peaches, or 6 large white peaches (to yield 4 cups sliced)
1 cup packed brown sugar
2 teaspoons vanilla extract
2 teaspoons salt
3 tablespoons all-purpose flour
1/4 cup (1/2 stick) unsalted butter, melted
Grated zest of 1 medium lemon

Juice of 1/2 lemon
5 tablespoons plus 1 teaspoon (2/3 stick) unsalted butter, melted
1 (5-ounce) can evaporated milk
1 cup all-purpose flour
1 tablespoon sugar
2 teaspoons baking powder
1 teaspoon salt
1/4 cup sugar

Slice the peaches into a 9x13-inch baking dish, allowing the juice to drip into the dish as well. Add the brown sugar, vanilla, 2 teaspoons salt, and 3 tablespoons flour, and mix well. Stir in 1/4 cup melted butter, the lemon zest, and lemon juice. Let stand while you make the topping, stirring occasionally.

For the topping, combine 2/3 stick butter, the evaporated milk, 1 cup flour, 1 tablespoon sugar, the baking powder, and 1 teaspoon salt in a bowl. Mix with a fork just until moist; do not overbeat. Using small portions of the mixture at a time, make little "biscuits" the size of ping pong balls. Place over the fruit in the baking dish.

Bake at 400 degrees for about 30 minutes or until all the little biscuits are browned. Let stand to cool. Sprinkle 1/4 cup sugar over the top of the biscuits.

Serves 6

For my husband's August 4 birthday, I like to serve three fruit cobblers with homemade vanilla ice cream. We had a really special friend and preacher over for Bill's birthday celebration years ago, and when I asked this spiritual giant if he would please say the blessing before our Sunday birthday lunch, he whispered to me: "I will, if you save me some of all of those cobblers." He didn't even know about the ice cream, and he really prayed over Bill when I told him that I would personally save him some of all three cobblers and a bowl of homemade vanilla ice cream, as well. I told you food is a blessing.

Fresh Pineapple Cobbler

Fresh pineapple is available year round, and we tend to forget how good it is when cooked. Pineapple baked with brown sugar and topped with a big meringue crust is just heaven to me. It's especially pretty in individual potpie ramekins, because everyone gets a lot of everything good, and no one scrapes the meringue off the top just as you get to the serving dish. At my house, just don't get in line behind my husband. He loads up on the part he likes best, and giving him his own ramekin makes everyone happy.

1¹/₂ cups packed dark brown sugar
4 cups fresh pineapple chunks (do not use canned)
1¹/₂ cups sugar
1¹/₂ cups all-purpose flour
2¹/₂ teaspoons baking powder
2 teaspoons salt
1¹/₂ cups (about) milk
¹/₂ cup (1 stick) unsalted butter, melted
Meringue Topping (page 113)

Combine the brown sugar and pineapple in a glass bowl, and mix well.

Combine the sugar, flour, baking powder, and salt in a large bowl. Add enough of the milk to moisten the big lump (it should be moist enough to almost pour over the fruit, like big damp biscuit dough, which it is).

Pour the melted butter into a 9x9-inch baking pan, spreading it evenly into the corners. Spoon the pineapple mixture over the butter. Top with the flour mixture.

Bake at 350 degrees for about 45 to 60 minutes or until the dough flakes when tested with a fork. Spoon the Meringue Topping over the warm cobbler, spreading all the way to the edges. Broil until the tips of the meringue are browned. Serve within 2 hours.

You can omit the meringue and serve the cobbler with sweetened whipped cream, if you prefer.

Serves 6 to 8

This cobbler can be baked and served in individual ramekins if you like. I prefer the 10-ounce size, but you can adjust each individual serving according to your needs. This recipe produces about two quarts (64 ounces) of finished cobbler. Divide the size of your ramekins accordingly. For example, if you use the 10-ounce ramekins, you will have six ramekins filled and four ounces left for the cook for educational/testing purposes, which, as you know, negates all calories.

Place the ramekins on a heavy baking sheet to bake them. Just before serving, reheat the ramekins, remove from the oven, and top with meringue. Bake at 500 degrees until the tips of the meringue are browned (watch them carefully). Serve warm.

It is easier and safer to brown the meringues in a 500-degree oven than to put them under the broiler as called for with the large baking dish. You will have better control over each ramekin in a hot oven than under the broiler.

Cherry Clafouti

Clafoutis are cobblers in reality, but actually a clafouti, which is a baked fruit gratin of sorts, is a little more of a pudding than a cobbler. The pudding effect absorbs more of the juices, which is important with things like fresh cherries, peaches, or strawberries, all of which produce a lot of liquid.

There are three kinds of fresh cherries that come in at slightly different seasons: the very dark red ones; the sour red ones; and the sweet cherries that are a beautiful mottled yellow. (Suppliers are listed on page 170 under Sources.)

The best way to stone cherries, in my opinion, is to use a funny little gadget that has a little handle that pops the stones out of the cherries and drops the stone into a little bucket and the cherry into a bowl. I use this gadget for olives, too, when I have a lot of olives to stone for breads or whatever.

I usually buy a whole case of cherries at one time, don a pair of rubber gloves, a black T-shirt (cherries really stain), put on a good video, and have at it. It usually takes me about two hours to do a whole case. You do have to stem the cherries, too; then wash the cherries and put them in the little gadget. To keep them nice and crisp, which to me is a very important part of their charm, I put them in wide-mouthed glass quart jars and cover them with very good vodka, the currant kind if I can find it. I put at least 3 cups of sugar in each quart jar of cherries. I refrigerate the marinating cherries in their jars and turn them every now and then for months, because the sugar has not been heated and it takes a good while for it to dissolve. (Heating the sugar cooks the cherries too much. I have tried it, and I prefer to let the sugar melt in its own good time. It will.)

3 cups stoned fresh cherries	4 eggs, beaten
1/2 cup sugar	1 1/2 cups sugar
2 tablespoons vanilla extract	2 teaspoons salt
1 1/2 cups milk	3/4 cup all-purpose flour
1/2 cup heavy cream	1/4 cup sugar

Combine the cherries, 1/2 cup sugar, and the vanilla in a bowl, and mix well. Marinate until baking time.

Combine the milk, cream, eggs, 1 1/2 cups sugar, the salt, and flour in a mixer bowl, and beat until smooth. Spread the cherry mixture in a lightly oiled 8x8-inch baking dish. Spoon the flour mixture over the cherries.

Bake at 350 degrees for about 1 hour or until a knife inserted near the center comes out clean. Remove from the oven, and sprinkle with 1/4 cup sugar. Let cool to room temperature. Serve with vanilla ice cream or whipped cream.

Makes about 6 servings

These marinated cherries are wonderful in clafoutis or cobblers; over any type of pound cake; or just out of the jar. The huge amount of vodka is offset by the huge amount of sugar. If your cherries taste too strong after a month or so, add sugar.

My good friends Chris and Idie Hastings mix some of the fruit, the liqueur it makes, and a lemon peel in white wine, sparkling or flat, for a fabulous summer spritzer. It is also good mixed with a little Perrier or ginger ale for a summer cooler.

I give these cherries in pretty glass bottles to special people at Christmas, because I am really giving away something I would rather keep for myself. That's what giving is all about, I'm sure, but I am selective about to whom I give my treasures. Idie and Chris, Nanci Chazen, and Bette and Finley McRae as of now are the only honored recipients. Bette and Finley send me cherries every year from Oregon, so I know they appreciate them. Nanci loves everything, and Idie and Chris have great ideas about how to enjoy these treasures. I hardly offer any to my own family. One narrowed eye and they are off my list.

Simple Swift Soufflé

The title of this soufflé is not a euphemism: It is so simple that you would never think it would work, but it really does. Everything that goes into any soufflé has to be fully cooked. This is especially important for a savory soufflé. If not fully cooked for a sweet soufflé, the fruit should be either puréed or chopped very small (else they will sink to the bottom and burn). Soufflés are, as you know, a lot of poof, so over-season them with spices and flavors, and don't forget a pinch or two of salt to bring out all the other flavors, whether sweet or savory.

1/4 cup sugar
2 tablespoons fresh lemon juice
8 egg yolks
Zest of 1 large orange
Zest of 1 large lemon
1 cup sugar
8 egg whites
2 teaspoons salt

Butter a 1-quart straight-sided soufflé dish, and sprinkle lightly with a small amount of sugar. Set aside.

Dissolve 1/4 cup sugar in the lemon juice. Combine with the egg yolks, orange zest, and lemon zest in a food processor, and mix well. Add 1 cup sugar, and process until all graininess has disappeared.

Beat the egg whites with the salt in the bowl of a heavy-duty mixer until they mound up and are like marshmallows. Do not beat until they are dry. If you do, beat in 1 more egg white to smooth it out.

Fold the egg whites and citrus mixture together in a bowl. Spoon into the prepared soufflé dish. Bake at 375 degrees for 22 minutes or until the soufflé is puffy and the center is almost set.

Serves 4 to 6

Grand Occasions

"Grand Occasions" can be anything from a simple get-together to a very elaborate birthday party. A Grand Occasion Dessert can be as simple as a dozen cupcakes on a three-tiered cake stand to an elaborate fondant-covered, multi-tiered, filled cake. There is, indeed, a wonderful childlikeness about desserts. (This is not at all "childishness," which is quite different and not at all appealing.) Desserts have about them something clean and pure that cuts across all age groups. Toddlers don't care too much for much else; older people in nursing homes usually get teary-eyed over a plate of warm cookies from home. Sick people in hospitals delight to get a box of homemade candies or cookies even if their own diets are restricted, because somehow it eases their own pain by urging others to "Go ahead . . . help yourself. My friend made them for me."

Desserts, I guess, are like anything else: All about people, and usually quite unabashedly so. "This is my friend Rose's white cake! You will never, ever have anything like it!" Such enthusiasm is usually not only not easily squelched; it usually is quite formidable. Just you TRY to interject that YOUR white cake is the best in the world, and see what happens.

Desserts, then, bring with them that wonderful quality that is so rapidly fading in our society today: That of fierce loyalty. We need that loyalty to what we love and to what comforts us. Because, hopefully, what comforts and cheers us will (and usually does) comfort and cheer others.

Desserts, either for "grand" or "lowly" occasions, tell us about ourselves, our families, our friends, and even about our enemies. ("She was a HARD woman. She didn't even like desserts.") Desserts are rewards and treats: hard to resist, and easy to take to excess. They are, however, in themselves rather self-limiting. Even the Book of Proverbs says that we dare not eat too much honey. Desserts can be hard work (sugar, chocolate, and some brides are notoriously cantankerous); curious; generous; and, of course, personal. Desserts are grand occasions and ordinary days.

*Our frou-frou days
of soufflés,
Of shimmery-shiny
custards and
crème brûlées;
Pâte a Choux Swans,
and Paris-Brests
Which sounded
then and now
Like a ballet at best.*

*We adored Floating
Islands in Spun
Sugar Cages,
Puff Pastry in its
myriad stages,
But have we learned
now what we must
have known then:
Gilding lilies
must be a sin.*

*Now it's yogurt
and fruit
And low-fat mirages;
Merely VISIONS
of sugar plums
Are allowed in
our barrages*

*Of Dreams of
the past,
And of hopes
that soon
We can return to find
Our sweet dreams
came true.*

Chocolate Cake and Icing

3 cups all-purpose flour, sifted
1 teaspoon baking soda
1 teaspoon salt
3/4 cup baking cocoa
1/2 cup boiling water
2 1/4 cups sugar

1 1/2 cups (3 sticks) unsalted butter,
   softened
4 eggs
1 cup milk
1 tablespoon vanilla extract
Chocolate Icing (below)

Lightly oil two 3x8-inch round cake pans. Line with lightly oiled waxed paper. Sift the flour, baking soda, and salt onto a sheet of waxed paper. Sift the cocoa into the boiling water, stirring until it forms a paste. Let stand to cool. Beat the sugar and butter in a mixer bowl for 4 to 5 minutes or until blended and smooth. Add the eggs one at a time, beating well and scraping the side of the bowl after each addition.

Mix the milk and vanilla in a small bowl. Add to the cocoa mixture, whisking until smooth. Add the flour mixture and the cocoa mixture alternately to the egg mixture, mixing well and scraping the side of the bowl occasionally after each addition. Spoon the batter into the prepared cake pans. Bang each pan on a hard surface to remove any air bubbles. Bake at 350 degrees for 25 to 30 minutes or until the cake tests done. Remove from the oven, and let cool in the pans for 10 minutes. Remove to a wire rack to cool completely.

Spread some of the Chocolate Icing over each layer. Assemble the cakes, pegging them as described on page 130. Be generous with the icing, especially as a filling between layers. Serve at room temperature.

Makes 12 servings

Chocolate Icing

2 cups whipping cream
4 cups (24 ounces) miniature
   semisweet chocolate chips

1 tablespoon light corn syrup

Bring the whipping cream almost to a boil in a saucepan. Melt the chocolate chips in a double boiler, stirring until smooth. Pour the cream over the melted chocolate, whisking constantly until the mixture smoothes out (it will). Blend in the corn syrup. Chill the mixture over a bowl of ice for 1 hour, whisking occasionally. The bottom of the mixture will get quite cold, and you want the entire mixture to get cold enough to set and become spreadable.

Makes about 6 cups

The cake pans called for here are three inches deep. You can use pans that are two inches deep, but then you will have to use three cake pans for this much batter. If you like a lot of layers on a cake (and thus a lot of icing), the three-inch pans produce two layers that can be split horizontally with a serrated knife, then iced. I find that it makes a much more moist cake to split the two layers into four, rather than using more cake pans. See pages 170–171 under Sources for the deeper cake pans. (They are also excellent for cheesecakes.)

There is no better name for this cake than what I have titled it.
It is an old-fashioned chocolate cake that my grandmother used to
make during the War years. My mother and my sister, Virginia,
and I lived with my grandparents during those years. My grandfather
was in the soft-drink business, so we had cocoa and sugar during
rationing, when no one else did.

I can remember as a child stirring the cocoa with the hot water and the
way that burst of cocoa smelled when they combined. There is still, to me,
no more wonderful fragrance. My grandfather's clothes always smelled like
chocolate and leather and vanilla. I will always love those woody
fragrances. The taste of this cake brings it all back, and I can think of no
greater gift to give or receive than this lovely delicious cake. I hope you
make it often. It's our family's favorite birthday cake. I must have fifteen
notes of the birthdays we baked this for each year.
This, to us, is what a birthday cake should be.

Coconut Layer Cake

4 cups sifted cake flour
1 teaspoon baking powder
1 teaspoon baking soda
2 teaspoons salt
6 eggs
1 tablespoon vanilla extract
1¹/₂ cups (3 sticks) unsalted butter,
    softened

2 cups sugar
1¹/₃ cups buttermilk
Coconut Filling (page 131)
Seven-Minute Marshmallow Icing
    (page 105)
Chocolate Sauce (page 131)

Lightly oil two 3x8-inch cake pans or three 2x9-inch pans. Line with lightly oiled waxed paper. Sift the flour, baking powder, baking soda, and salt onto a sheet of waxed paper. Mix the eggs and vanilla in a small bowl.

Cream the butter and sugar in a mixer bowl for 5 minutes or until light and fluffy. (You cannot over-cream these two ingredients before you add the flour.) Add the egg mixture gradually, beating well after each addition and scraping the side of the bowl occasionally. Add the flour mixture and the buttermilk alternately, beating at low speed after each addition and scraping the side of the bowl occasionally. Beat at medium speed until mixed but no longer than 2 minutes.

Spoon the batter into the cake pans, and bang each pan on a hard surface to settle the batter and remove any air bubbles. Bake at 350 degrees for 35 to 45 minutes or until the layers test done. Do not overbake. Remove from the oven, and let cool in the pans for 10 minutes. Unmold onto a wire rack, and remove the waxed paper. Let stand until completely cooled.

Trim the browned crusts from the layers with a serrated knife (particularly on the sides, but the bottoms and tops as well, if necessary). Spread cooled Coconut Filling between the cake layers, stacking each layer carefully. Insert 4 long drinking straws, very thin dowels (¹/₁₆ inch), or long kabob spears into the layers from top to bottom. (This is to keep the layers from sliding. Place each straw at least 2 inches from the edge of the cake and several inches apart around and through the layers. Dowels that are too close to the edges will tear the cake apart. Without the dowels, the layers will slide apart. If that happens, call it a trifle.) Trim the dowels as necessary with poultry scissors.

Spread Seven-Minute Marshmallow Icing over the top and side of the cake. Refrigerate until serving time. Serve with Chocolate Sauce.

Makes 12 servings

In the wonderful movie When Harry Met Sally, *the outtakes at the end included a wacky dialogue between Meg Ryan and Billy Crystal about the wedding cake that they had for their eventual (and inevitable) wedding. They had a coconut cake "with a wonderful chocolate sauce on the side, because you don't want too much sauce, you know."*

The coconut cake with chocolate sauce here is incredibly fabulous. I pool the chocolate sauce on the dessert plate, cut a real slice of coconut cake, and I keep the chocolate sauce nearby. Our family does want "too much"; in fact, we really overdo it with the chocolate sauce. That's why we don't look like Meg Ryan (maybe).

Coconut Filling

6 eggs, beaten
1 cup sugar
1 teaspoon salt
1½ cups milk or canned coconut
   milk
1½ cups heavy cream

3 tablespoons flour
2 teaspoons vanilla extract
2 tablespoons unflavored gelatin
½ cup cold water
1 cup boiling water
2 cups sweetened coconut

Beat the eggs, sugar, salt, milk, cream, and flour in a double boiler. Cook over boiling water for about 10 minutes or until the mixture is thick and coats a spoon, whisking frequently. Let cool to room temperature. Stir in the vanilla.

Soften the gelatin in ½ cup cold water. Add the boiling water, stirring until the gelatin is dissolved and the mixture is clear and still warm. Add 1 cup of the milk mixture to the gelatin, and mix well. Stir the gelatin mixture into the remaining milk mixture. (The temperature of the milk mixture and the gelatin should be approximately the same. If one is hot and the other cold, the gelatin will become stringy; you would need to strain it out and start over.) Add the coconut, and mix well. Cover with plastic wrap or waxed paper (it should touch the custard itself to prevent a skin from forming). Let cool until almost set but still spreadable.

Makes about 3 cups

Chocolate Sauce

1 cup baking cocoa
2 cups sugar
2 cups light corn syrup
1 cup heavy cream
6 tablespoons unsalted butter
2 teaspoons salt

Bring the baking cocoa, sugar, corn syrup, cream, butter, and salt to a boil in a saucepan. Cook for 4 minutes, stirring constantly. This sauce keeps well in the refrigerator in a 1-quart glass Mason jar.

Makes about 4 cups

Lemon Meringue Cake

The Cipriani restaurants in New York and Venice always have the best desserts imaginable out on a sideboard, so that they are the first things you see when you enter Arrigo's restaurants. (Well, it's the first thing I always see there.) My two favorites are a vanilla meringue cake and a very thin lemon tart.

These desserts drive me crazy, but I have finally figured out how to handle the frustrations they give me: I order just one white peach and Prosecco Bellini. (That's really hard to do. I would prefer about three of them, but I have learned over the years how to do this dessert thing.) Then I order a plain grilled fish, a green salad, and a very few roasted potatoes. No wonderful Italian breadsticks, none of their fabulous rolls (I told you these two desserts are great).

Then, I order two desserts: the lemon tart and the meringue cake. Yes, two, both for me. I have tried sharing them with Kris, my sweet and generous daughter-in-law; my granddaughter, Chloe; my husband, Bill (forget it); and even my skinny friend Nanci Chazen. It does not work. They do not share right. They all (even sweet, generous little Chloe) only give me one tiny little taste of theirs, and then they take a lot of mine.

When I am at home, dreaming of Italy, far from New York, I don't want to bake both desserts, so I put the two together in this Lemon Meringue Cake. Then I dream about the next wonderful time when I can visit Cipriani's again.

4 cups sifted cake flour
1 teaspoon baking powder
1 teaspoon baking soda
2 teaspoons salt
6 eggs
1 tablespoon vanilla extract
2 cups sugar

1½ cups (3 sticks) unsalted butter, softened
1⅓ cups buttermilk
Lemon Filling (page 133)
Swiss Meringue Icing (sidebar, page 133)

Lightly oil two 3x8-inch cake pans or three 2x9-inch pans. Line with lightly oiled waxed paper. Sift the flour, baking powder, baking soda, and salt onto a sheet of waxed paper. Mix the eggs and vanilla in a small bowl.

Cream the sugar and butter in a mixer bowl for 5 minutes or until light and fluffy. (You cannot over-cream these two ingredients before you add the flour.) Add the egg mixture gradually, beating well after each addition and scraping the side of the bowl occasionally. Add the flour mixture and the buttermilk alternately, beating at low speed after each addition and scraping the side of the bowl occasionally. Beat at medium speed until mixed but no longer than 2 minutes.

The use of uncooked, or even partially cooked, egg whites has led many manufacturers of dried egg whites to produce their products for the general consumer, whereas previously the dried egg whites were available only through commercial food distributors and in great quantities.

Some of the products in the grocery stores are quite good and reliable, but some taste very sour and do not produce a good meringue. Brand names change constantly, so ask a commercial baker whose product he or she recommends, or try them out yourself on small cookies or muffins before using them on a large cake.

If you bake meringues often, commercial food distributors also sell pasteurized egg whites that are frozen in half-gallon cartons like the ones milk comes in. They are a very good product, and, since they are pasteurized, they are labeled "safe."

Lemon Meringue Cake *(continued)*

Spoon the batter into the cake pans, and bang each pan on a hard surface to settle the batter and remove any air bubbles. Bake at 350 degrees for 35 to 45 minutes or until the layers test done. Do not overbake. Remove from the oven, and let cool in the pans for 10 minutes. Unmold onto a wire rack, and remove the waxed paper. Let stand until completely cooled.

Trim the browned crusts from the layers with a serrated knife (particularly on the sides, but the bottoms and tops as well, if necessary). Spread cooled Lemon Filling between the cake layers, stacking each layer carefully. Insert 4 long drinking straws, very thin dowels (1/16 inch), or long kabob spears into the layers from top to bottom. (This is to keep the layers from sliding. Place each straw at least 2 inches from the edge of the cake and several inches apart around and through the layers. Dowels that are too close to the edges will tear the cake apart. Without the dowels, the layers will slide apart. If that happens, call it a trifle.) Trim the dowels as necessary with poultry scissors.

Spread Swiss Meringue Icing over the top and side of the cake. Refrigerate until serving time.

Makes 12 servings

Lemon Filling

1 cup (2 sticks) unsalted butter
2 cups sugar
Juice of 4 large lemons

6 eggs, beaten
1/2 teaspoon salt

Combine the butter, sugar, and lemon juice in a double boiler. Cook over medium heat just until the butter is melted; do not boil. Add the eggs and salt. Cook until the mixture is thick and coats a spoon, stirring frequently. Pour into a bowl. (If any of the eggs cooked at all, strain the entire mixture into a glass bowl.) Place plastic wrap directly on the top of the filling to prevent a skin from forming. Let cool over a bowl of ice, stirring occasionally. Refrigerate until needed. (It will spread better when it is very cold.)

Makes about 4 cups

For Swiss Meringue Icing, combine 1 cup egg whites (about 8), 2 teaspoons cream of tartar, 2 cups sugar, and 2 teaspoons salt in a heatproof metal mixer bowl. Place the bowl over barely simmering water. Whisk constantly until the sugar is dissolved and the mixture is hot to the touch (but not hot enough to cook the egg whites). Using the whisk attachment to the mixer, beat at high speed until the mixture resembles marshmallow creme. Add 2 teaspoons vanilla extract, whisking quickly to avoid deflating the egg whites.

Makes about 1 cup

Limoncello Cake

4 cups all-purpose flour
1 teaspoon (rounded) baking
    powder
1 teaspoon salt
Grated zest of 3 large lemons
Juice of 2 large lemons
    (about $1/4$ cup)

$1/2$ cup water
$1/2$ cup (1 stick) unsalted butter,
    softened
$2^1/2$ cups sugar
5 eggs
Limoncello Syrup (below)

This cake is wonderful with sweetened berries, especially fresh blueberries. Sweetened whipped cream is also excellent against the lemon flavor. Add $1/4$ cup confectioners' sugar and 1 tablespoon vanilla extract to 1 cup whipping cream. Beat until thickened; do not overbeat. Pile the whipped cream in the center of the cake, and arrange the sweetened berries or other fruit around the edges of the serving platter.

Sift the flour, baking powder, and salt together. Mix the lemon zest, lemon juice, and water in a bowl. Cream the butter and sugar at medium speed in a large mixer bowl. Add the eggs one at a time, beating well after each addition and scraping the side of the bowl occasionally. Add the flour mixture and lemon juice mixture alternately, beating at low speed after each addition. Beat at medium speed for 1 to 2 minutes or just until mixed; do not overbeat. Spoon the batter into a well-oiled bundt cake pan or baba mold. Bang the pan on a hard surface to level the batter and rid it of air bubbles. Bake at 350 degrees for 45 to 60 minutes or until the cake tests done.

Let cool in the pan for 10 minutes. Unmold onto a wire rack to cool completely. Remove to a shallow platter. Poke small holes in the cake with a long kabob skewer or a very thin dowel. Ladle the warm Limoncello Syrup over the cake. (Discard the lemon slices if they are no longer attractive enough to use for a garnish.) The excess syrup will collect on the platter. Spoon the excess syrup over the cake at intervals to infuse the cake with the syrup. Serve at room temperature. Garnish with lemon slices, mint leaves, and fresh strawberries.

Makes 12 servings

Limoncello Syrup

1 cup hot water
2 cups sugar
3 lemons, each cut into 6 to 8 slices
1 cup limoncello liqueur, or $1/2$ cup fresh lemon juice

Bring the hot water to a boil in a saucepan. Add the sugar, and cook for about 4 minutes, stirring constantly until the sugar is dissolved. Remove from the heat. Add the lemon slices and limoncello. Let stand to steep while the cake cools.

Makes about 3 cups

Lemons from southern Italy are nothing like the lemons that we get in the markets here in the United States. I have grown lemons in my yard and now on my patio here in the States that were just as sweet and big as the Italian ones, but only in a limited number.

The only way to bring lemons back from Italy is as limoncello, a wonderful lemon liqueur that comes from several places in the south of Italy. "La migliore?" always brings the shopkeeper running to present me with a bottle of limoncello that I would never have chosen. "The best?" always gives Italians the opportunity that they so love: to correct you and set you straight. Especially in Tuscany, and particularly in Florence, where we usually rent an apartment and stumble through our Italian classes whenever we get the chance. The Florentines love to teach and correct and take time with you. If you can, try different brands of limoncello there in Italy, and you will probably find that they were absolutely right about "la migliore."

Orange Bavarian Cake

*In January, my sister and her husband send us giant juicy tangelos
called Honey Bells. The company in Florida sends two bibs with the fruit
to protect the eater from the juice! After we have eaten our way through
half the case, I juice the Honey Bells with an electric juicer.
What we don't drink outright, I use for this cake.*

*You will notice that this cake calls for very little orange or tangerine juice.
We must need all that citrus juice with its potassium and vitamin C every
winter. We sure do enjoy it, and I bet we just glow.*

*I have listed the company on page 171 under Sources. A word to the wise:
You had better order them very early, or you won't get them. They have a
limited number and many, many repeat customers.*

I have listed the company on page 171 under Sources.

1 tablespoon yeast
$1/8$ teaspoon sugar
$1/2$ cup warm milk
$1 3/4$ cups all-purpose flour
2 eggs, beaten
1 teaspoon salt
$1/4$ cup ($1/2$ stick) unsalted butter
3 tablespoons sugar

Grated zest of 2 large oranges
  or tangerines
  (about 3 tablespoons)
1 cup fresh orange or tangerine
  juice
1 cup sugar
Juice of $1/2$ lemon
Orange Bavarian (page 137)

Combine the yeast, $1/8$ teaspoon sugar, and milk in a bowl, stirring until
the sugar is dissolved. Combine the flour, eggs, salt, and yeast mixture in
a mixer bowl. With the mixer at low speed, add the butter, 3 tablespoons
sugar, and the orange zest. Beat at medium speed for about 6 to
8 minutes or until the dough begins to leave the side of the bowl. Shape
the dough into a ball, and place it in a lightly oiled bowl. Let rise,
covered with a warm cloth, for about 2 hours or until doubled in bulk.

For the syrup, combine the orange juice, 1 cup sugar, and the lemon
juice in a saucepan. Cook over medium heat, stirring until the sugar is
dissolved. Increase the heat. Boil for about 3 minutes or until slightly
syrupy. Let stand to cool.

Punch down the dough; shape it into a circle. Place in a well-oiled bundt
pan or large round baba pan. Pinch the ends together so that it is seamless.
Let rise in a warm place for about 1 hour or until doubled in bulk. Bake
at 350 degrees for 30 to 40 minutes or until the cake tests done. Cool in
the pan for 10 minutes. Remove to a wire rack. Before the cake is cooled,
place it on a platter with sides. Reheat the syrup. Ladle the warm syrup
over the cake several times, reusing the pooled syrup at the bottom of
the platter. Garnish with fresh berries or pretty slices of fresh oranges or
tangerines (remove the seeds first). Serve with the Orange Bavarian.

Makes 12 servings

*I have a straight-sided
glass soufflé dish that
fits exactly in the
center of my large
finished baba cake. If
the cake rises too
much in the center
while baking, I trim
out the center a bit
and fit the finished
molded Bavarian in
its glass dish down
inside the cake. It
makes a very pretty
presentation. You can
always make small
molds of the Bavarian
in individual custard
cups or lightly oiled
muffin cups, and turn
them out either onto a
large serving platter
around the cake or
individually onto each
dessert plate and pass
the cake separately.*

Orange Bavarian

3 egg yolks
$1/3$ cup sugar
$1/2$ cup milk
$1/2$ cup heavy cream
2 envelopes unflavored gelatin
$1/2$ cup cold orange juice or tangerine juice
$1/2$ cup boiling water
2 teaspoons vanilla extract

Beat the egg yolks and sugar at high speed in a mixer bowl until pale yellow. Bring the milk and cream almost to a boil in a saucepan. Add a small amount of the milk mixture at a time to the egg mixture, beating at low speed until the sugar is dissolved.

Soften the gelatin in the cold orange juice. Add the boiling water, stirring until the gelatin is dissolved and the mixture is clear. While it is still warm, stir in about $1/2$ cup of the warm egg mixture; stir the gelatin mixture into the remaining egg mixture. Stir in the vanilla.

Pour into a decorative 1-quart glass mold. Refrigerate overnight. Garnish with orange or tangerine slices.

Makes about 2 cups

White Chocolate Mousse Cake

Melting white chocolate can be tricky. It has a very low burning point, and therefore it must be melted very slowly over very low heat in a double boiler. It should be over very hot, but not boiling, water.

I do not like to use the microwave for melting chocolate, because it is difficult to stop the melting process without constantly watching the chocolate. Keep the chocolate stirred with a fork, scraping up from the very bottom where the heat over a double boiler is the greatest. There is no remedy for even slightly scorched chocolate, especially the white, so watch it carefully.

It is very important when combining the cream cheese mixture and gelatin mixture that each be at about the same temperature. Gelatin will become stringy if it is plunged into a very cold mixture, and there will be no remedy. Each mixture should be a little warmer than body temperature (about 100 degrees) when you mix them together.

1 (9-inch) Chocolate Cake (page 128)
12 ounces cream cheese, softened
1/2 cup confectioners' sugar
Grated zest and juice of 1 medium orange
1 tablespoon orange liqueur, such as Triple Sec, Grand Marnier, or
    Cointreau; or 2 teaspoons orange extract
2 teaspoons vanilla extract
2 tablespoons unflavored gelatin
2 cups cold heavy cream
5 ounces white chocolate, melted
Chocolate Glaze (page 139)

Slice each cake layer horizontally into two thin layers with a serrated knife.

For the mousse, beat the cream cheese, confectioners' sugar, orange zest, orange juice, liqueur, and vanilla in a mixer bowl until blended and smooth. Soften the gelatin in the cream in a saucepan. Heat over very low heat, stirring constantly until the gelatin is dissolved. Add the melted white chocolate, stirring until blended.

Stir about 1 cup of the cream cheese mixture into the warm gelatin mixture; stir the warm gelatin mixture into the remaining cream cheese mixture. Beat at low speed until very well combined.

Spread the mousse between the cake layers. Insert long kabob skewers or long cocktail forks at least 2 inches from the outside edge of the cake. Use 4 thin skewers or cocktail forks near the very center of the cake to keep the layers from sliding.

White Chocolate Mousse Cake (continued)

Line a 3x9-inch round cake pan with plastic wrap that extends at least 5 inches out of the pan in an "X" shape. (These extensions will provide handles for moving the cake later.)

Place the filled layers in the prepared cake pan. Cover the top of the cake with the plastic wrap handles. Chill for at least 4 hours or overnight.

Unmold the cake by pulling the handles; place on a serving platter. Drizzle with the warm Chocolate Glaze, or top with sweetened whipped cream.

Makes 12 servings

Chocolate Glaze

1 cup semisweet chocolate chips
$1/2$ cup (1 stick) unsalted butter
1 tablespoon light corn syrup

Combine the chocolate, butter, and corn syrup in a double boiler. Cook over medium heat until the chocolate and butter are melted and the mixture is shiny and glossy, stirring constantly.

Makes about 1 cup

Lady Baltimore Pavé

A pavé is a square or rectangular pan that makes something of a brick shape. You probably have to use your imagination to come up with a square brick, but the rectangular brick shape is a very nice shape with which to work. I use a one-pound or even larger loaf pan or cake pan for the cake. Then you can slice it horizontally, fill it, and reassemble it. It slices beautifully and looks lovely on a dessert plate with all its colors and stripes.

This is a rather classic French cake that is too often neglected today. It can also be made with three rectangular puff pastry sheets; with baked phyllo sheets; or even with meringues shaped into three flat rectangles, filled, and then reassembled.

The recipe and technique here uses the cake and its old-fashioned lemon and fruit filling known as "Lady Baltimore." Since I have two adorable granddaughters in Baltimore, I refer to it in our family as my Katherine-Annie Cake. It is almost as pretty as they are.

Katherine and Anne, my Baltimore grandchildren, have no idea what a real Lady Baltimore Cake is, so, when I make this for them, I omit the traditional dried figs and pecans that the original recipe calls for. Instead, I use a lemon curd lightened with whipped cream to make a lemon mousse, and for the fruit I use dried cherries, cranberries, and golden raisins. It makes a very pretty filling for two very pretty girls.

1$^{1}/_{3}$ cups cake flour
2 teaspoons baking powder
1 teaspoon salt
$^{1}/_{4}$ cup ($^{1}/_{2}$ stick) unsalted butter, softened
$^{3}/_{4}$ cup sugar

1 teaspoon vanilla extract
1 egg, beaten
$^{1}/_{2}$ cup milk
Lemon Mousse (page 141)
Whipped Cream Icing (page 141)

Sift the flour, baking powder, and salt onto a sheet of waxed paper. Cream the butter and sugar in a mixer bowl until light and fluffy. Add the vanilla and egg, and mix well. Add the flour mixture and the milk alternately, beating after each addition and scraping the side of the bowl occasionally. Do not overbeat.

Spoon the batter into a well-oiled and paper-lined 1-pound loaf pan. Bang the pan on a hard surface to level the batter and remove any air bubbles. Bake at 350 degrees for about 25 to 30 minutes or until the cake tests done.

Cool in the pan for 10 minutes. Unmold onto a wire rack to cool completely. Cut the loaf horizontally into thirds with a serrated knife. Spread chilled Lemon Mousse between the bottom two layers. Chill in the refrigerator. (If the layers seem to be sliding, peg the layers together with long cocktail forks or kabob skewers trimmed with scissors. Peg it at each end and in the center.) Spread Whipped Cream Icing (or Seven-Minute Marshmallow Icing, page 105) over the top and side of the cake.

Makes 12 servings

Lemon Mousse

1/2 cup (1 stick) unsalted butter, softened
1 1/2 cups sugar
4 eggs, beaten
Grated zest and juice of 3 large lemons
2 cups whipping cream, whipped
1 cup any one or any combination of mixed chopped dried fruits, such
    as cherries, cranberries, and golden raisins; or mixed chopped dried
    fruits with chopped pecans or almonds
1 cup sweetened coconut (optional)

Combine the butter and sugar in a nonreactive saucepan. Cook over
low heat until the butter is melted and the sugar is dissolved, stirring
constantly. Let cool slightly. Add the eggs, whisking constantly to keep
the eggs from scrambling. Add the lemon zest and lemon juice. Cook
over medium heat for about 10 minutes or until the mixture is thick and
coats a spoon, stirring frequently. Remove from the heat. Pour into a
bowl. (If any of the eggs did scramble, strain the mixture through a
sieve into a glass bowl.) Place plastic wrap directly on top of the custard.
Chill until the custard is very cold and set. The custard can be made up
to a week ahead and kept in a tightly capped glass jar in the refrigerator.
Fold the whipped cream, dried fruit, and coconut into the cold custard,
and mix gently.

Makes about 3 cups

Whipped Cream Icing

2 cups whipping cream
1/4 cup confectioners' sugar
1 tablespoon vanilla extract

Beat the whipping cream, confectioners' sugar, and vanilla in a mixer
bowl until stiff enough to ice the cake.

Makes about 3 cups

Peaches and Cream Pavé

3 cups all-purpose flour, sifted
1 tablespoon (scant) baking powder
1 teaspoon baking soda
1 teaspoon salt
1 cup (2 sticks) unsalted butter, softened
2 cups sugar
4 eggs, beaten
1¼ cups buttermilk

2 teaspoons vanilla extract
3 cups whipping cream
3 tablespoons confectioners' sugar
1 tablespoon vanilla extract
2 cups peeled and sliced fresh peaches, cut into 1-inch pieces
1 peach, peeled, cut into 8 pretty slices, for garnish
Fresh mint, for garnish

Lightly oil a 9x13-inch baking pan. Line with lightly oiled waxed paper. Set aside. Sift the flour, baking powder, baking soda, and salt together, and set aside.

Cream the butter and sugar in a large mixer bowl for 6 to 8 minutes or until blended and smooth. Add the beaten eggs gradually, mixing after each addition and scraping the side of the bowl occasionally. Beat at high speed until the mixture is light and fluffy. Add the flour mixture and buttermilk alternately, beating after each addition and scraping the side of the bowl frequently. Stir in 2 teaspoons vanilla. (Do not overbeat once the flour has been added.)

Spoon the batter into the prepared pan. Bang the pan on a hard surface to level the batter and remove any air bubbles. Bake at 350 degrees for about 30 to 45 minutes or until the cake tests done. Bake at 325 degrees if you are using a glass baking dish.

Cool in the pan for 10 minutes. Unmold onto a lightly oiled baking sheet or a treated paper rectangle made for cakes. Let stand to cool completely.

Beat the whipped cream, confectioners' sugar, and 1 tablespoon vanilla in a mixer bowl until of a spreadable consistency.

Cut the cake lengthwise into two even rectangles with a serrated knife. Spread the bottom layer with some of the sweetened whipped cream. Spoon the peaches evenly over the whipped cream. Top with the other rectangle. (If the cake seems to slide, peg the two ends and the middle with trimmed long cocktail picks or kabob skewers to anchor the layers.)

Spread the remaining whipped cream over the top and side of the cake. Place the peach slices down the center of the finished cake. Garnish with fresh mint.

Makes 12 servings

Raspberry Pavlova

Pavlova, the famous Russian dancer, did us all a favor by loving the meringue and fruit dessert named for her. In today's low-fat diets, meringues reign as much as any monarchy, past or present. A "pavlova" is an odd combination of events: The meringue is baked until it is dried out and crisp, then filled with a sweetened cream until it becomes like marshmallows. Oddly enough, there is no skipping steps to get back to the original creamy texture of the unbaked meringue.

2 cups fresh raspberries, rinsed and dried
1/4 cup sugar
1 tablespoon cornstarch
1 tablespoon white vinegar
1 tablespoon vanilla extract
1 cup egg whites (about 8), at room temperature
1 teaspoon salt
2 cups superfine sugar, or granulated sugar ground to superfine
  in a food processor
2 cups whipping cream
3 tablespoons confectioners' sugar
1 tablespoon vanilla extract
1 cup Chocolate Sauce (page 131)

Marinate the raspberries in 1/4 cup sugar for 1 hour or longer. Mix the cornstarch, vinegar, and 1 tablespoon vanilla in a bowl. Beat the egg whites and salt in a mixer bowl until soft peaks form. Beat in the superfine sugar 1 tablespoon at a time. Fold in the cornstarch mixture. Shape into a 9-inch circle on a foil-lined ungreased 10x15-inch baking pan, building up the sides about 2 inches. A large kitchen spoon slightly dampened with water makes this easier to shape.

Bake at 250 degrees for 1 to 1 1/2 hours or until you can gently push the meringue completely loose from the foil. It should not brown; if it begins to, lower the oven temperature and extend the baking time. Cool on a wire rack. Beat the whipping cream, confectioners' sugar, and 1 tablespoon vanilla in a mixer bowl until soft peaks form. Spoon into the baked meringue. Chill until serving time. Spoon the undrained raspberries evenly over the whipped cream. Serve the Chocolate Sauce separately in a glass pitcher.

Serves 8

There are numerous variations of the classic Pavlova. Lemon Filling (see Lemon Meringue Cake, page 133) and any sweetened berries; chocolate custard, strawberries, toasted almonds, and chocolate sauce; sweetened whipped cream, sweetened coconut, and chocolate sauce with toasted almonds; sweetened whipped cream and brandied cherries. These are only a few.

The meringue shapes are limited only by your imagination. I have made them in little swans on a pool of chocolate sauce and guava (or berry) sauce ("coulis," for the French among us) for wedding luncheons and showers.

Once the cream and the meringue get together, the result is creamy, thus preventing the occurrence of a shattering crash and a skittering meringue. Such a scary occurrence comes from assembling the dessert at the last minute. The finished dessert should be a very creamy texture by serving time. Remember that. Men especially hate crashing, skittering food.

Floating Island

2 cups egg whites (about 12 to 14)
2 teaspoons salt
1 teaspoon cream of tartar
1³/4 cups sugar
1 tablespoon vanilla extract
8 egg yolks
1 cup sugar
1/8 teaspoon salt
1 cup milk
1 cup heavy cream
1 tablespoon vanilla extract
3 tablespoons unsalted butter
Caramel Sugar Crown (page 145)

For the meringue, beat the egg whites, 2 teaspoons salt, and the cream of tartar at low speed in a large mixer bowl just until beginning to foam. Increase the speed to medium-high, and add 1³/4 cups sugar 1 tablespoon at a time, beating constantly until the meringue resembles marshmallow creme. Beat in 1 tablespoon vanilla. Spoon into a lightly oiled 4-quart glass soufflé dish with straight sides.

Bake at 250 degrees for 35 to 40 minutes or until a skewer inserted near the center comes out clean. The meringue should look puffed and shiny. Let cool in the soufflé dish on a wire rack. Chill until serving time. (If covered with plastic, it will keep for several days in the refrigerator.)

For the custard, beat the egg yolks, 1 cup sugar, and 1/8 teaspoon salt in a food processor or large mixer bowl until pale yellow. Combine the milk and cream in a saucepan, and bring almost to a boil. Add the hot milk mixture to the egg yolks with the food processor running. Be careful not to cook the eggs. Remove to a saucepan.

Cook over very low heat until the custard is thick and coats a spoon, stirring constantly. Be sure to scrape and stir all over the saucepan, including the edges. Remove from the heat. Add 1 tablespoon vanilla and the butter, and mix well. Adjust the amount of salt and/or vanilla if needed. Pour into a bowl. Place plastic wrap directly on the surface of the custard to prevent a skim from forming. (If the custard cooked the eggs at all, strain it into a glass bowl.) Chill thoroughly.

Serve the custard alongside the large island still in its baking dish; or spoon custard onto a platter with sides, and unmold the meringue island onto the pool of custard. Spin the Caramel Sugar Crown over the top. Serve any extra custard in a small glass pitcher.

Serves 6 to 8

Caramel Sugar Crown

2 cups sugar
$^2/_3$ cup boiling water

Combine the sugar and boiling water in a saucepan, stirring off heat until the sugar is completely dissolved. (Do not use a black-lined saucepan; you cannot see the color of the caramel as it hardens.) Cover the saucepan with a heavy lid, and bring the mixture to a boil. Wet a clean paintbrush or pastry brush with cold water, and wash down the side of the saucepan to keep the sugar from crystallizing. (Do not stir the syrup, either, or the sugar will crystallize.)

Watch carefully as large bubbles begin to form, which indicate it is near the caramel stage. Remove carefully from the heat just as it begins to caramelize; it is exceedingly and dangerously hot. Keep away from the edge of the counter to avoid spills. To spin caramel threads, use a fork to spread the caramel over the finished island and the cream. The caramel will harden as soon as it hits the cold meringue or custard.

Floating Island is a baked or poached meringue served in a pourable custard pool. It is often topped with a beautiful caramelized sugar cage. I bake the "island," that is, the meringue, if I have a particularly large group, or I poach individual large spoonfuls of meringue if I don't have too many guests or too much time.

These little meringues are a lot stronger than their appearance indicates. Back in my catering days, I packed up an enormous batch of about a million individual poached islands in their custard, in a huge, covered Tupperware-type container, packed in ice. I drove too fast for 114 miles in my straight-shift Honda Civic wagon over rocky, hilly terrain to a very important international Board meeting of a very important corporation. The islands and I arrived with time to spare and not in the least bit harmed. Obviously, they are like caterers in their deceptive appearance—tough little birds.

To make individual islands, instead of baking the meringue, use a large skillet with deep sides or a saucepan to poach the meringues. Fill the skillet with water and 1 teaspoon vinegar. Bring to a boil; reduce the heat immediately. Place any size islands in the water to poach. You can use egg-size, orange-size, or, my favorite, tennis-ball size meringues. Poach until you can see that they are cooked on one side. Turn them gently with a slotted spoon. Poach until done. Remove to a clean dish towel to drain. Place them in a large serving dish. Serve with the custard and the spun-sugar caramel threads. This makes about 24 tennis ball-size meringues.

Chocolate Cheesecake

Cheesecakes are still the number one dessert in America, having replaced apple pie years ago. I prefer a cheesecake without a crust, because, after all, a cheesecake is really a baked custard. The chocolate cheesecake here, though, does have a crust, but you don't have to use it if you like your custards plain, too. Be sure to use a lightly oiled waxed paper or parchment paper lining in the pan to facilitate removing the cheesecake. This recipe makes wonderful individual cheesecakes in tall-sided four- or six-inch ramekins. (You don't have to line the smaller ones with paper, but you do have to oil them to make them easier to unmold.)

1 baked Chocolate Crust (optional) (page 147)
24 ounces cream cheese, softened
1 1/2 cups sugar
1 cup sour cream
1 tablespoon vanilla extract
3 eggs, beaten
1/2 cup baking cocoa, sifted
2 tablespoons all-purpose flour
Chocolate Glaze (page 147)

Prepare and bake the Chocolate Crust as directed on page 147. If you are omitting the crust, lightly oil a 3x8-inch cake pan. Line with waxed paper.

Combine the cream cheese and sugar in the large bowl of a heavy-duty mixer, and beat until blended and smooth. Add the sour cream, vanilla, and eggs, and beat well. Add the baking cocoa and flour, and beat well.

Spoon into the prepared crust (or directly into the pan). Set the cake pan into a larger pan, and place them in the oven. Fill the larger pan with enough hot water to come halfway up the side of the cake pan.

Bake at 325 degrees for 1 hour and 20 minutes or until a knife inserted near the center comes out almost clean. The custard will continue to cook when removed from the oven.

Remove the cheesecake pan carefully from the hot water. Leave the water bath in the oven to cool down separately. This is safer than trying to remove both pans at once, with the bottom one full of boiling water.

Cool in the pan on a wire rack for about 1 hour. Chill, covered with plastic wrap, in the refrigerator overnight.

For cheesecakes, I prefer to use 3x8-inch cake pans rather than springform pans, because I always bake cheesecakes in a water bath. Obviously, a springform pan doesn't work as well even if it is lined on the outside with foil.

The three-inch-deep pans are available at very good kitchen and housewares stores, and I have listed a few on pages 170–171 under Sources. A 3x8-inch pan fits exactly into the next larger size cake pan (3x10-inch).

I use these deep pans for all my cakes, too. The finished layers can be sliced horizontally into as many as three layers each. These make cakes that are moister than those that are baked in many separate layers.

Chocolate Cheesecake *(continued)*

Spray a serving platter lightly with oil. To remove the cheesecake from the pan, loosen the side gently with a spatula or flat table knife. Invert the cheesecake onto the prepared serving platter. Tap the center of the pan to ensure that the cheesecake loosens from the pan. If you have used a crust, you will need to right the cheesecake onto the platter.

Pour the Chocolate Glaze over the cheesecake. Tilt the cheesecake to allow the glaze to drizzle down the side naturally.

Serves 8 to 10

Chocolate Glaze

1 cup semisweet chocolate chips
1 tablespoon vegetable shortening

Melt the chocolate chips and shortening in a saucepan, stirring until blended and smooth.

Makes about 1 cup

Chocolate Crust

1¹/2 cups shortbread crumbs (Lorna Doone-type cookies)
¹/4 cup sugar
¹/4 cup baking cocoa
¹/4 cup (¹/2 stick) unsalted butter, melted

Lightly oil a 3x8-inch cake pan. Line the pan with waxed paper. Combine the cookie crumbs, sugar, baking cocoa, and butter in a bowl, and mix well. Press onto the bottom and 1 inch up the side of the prepared pan.

Bake at 350 degrees for 8 minutes. Remove from the oven, and let cool completely before adding a filling.

Makes 1 crust

Grand Marnier Soufflé

*Some soufflés are made with a flour and butter mixture; then the egg
yolks are added, and finally the beaten egg whites are folded in.
Such soufflés are a lot more stable than those without a flour/butter
mixture. Nevertheless, the kind of soufflé that I have here is so
simple and quick that you should use it often just to stare down any
unfounded fears of soufflés that you may have acquired over the years.
Just be sure that anything that goes into a soufflé is already cooked,
because all you are doing is fluffing things up with egg whites.
You are not cooking any of the added ingredients.*

*Another thing to remember about any food with lots of egg whites is that
you have to season and flavor a great deal more than you normally would.*

*Children especially seem to like dessert soufflés. For them, you can
substitute frozen orange juice concentrate for the Grand Marnier.*

8 egg yolks
2/3 cup sugar
1/2 cup Grand Marnier or undiluted frozen orange juice concentrate
10 egg whites
1/2 teaspoon cream of tartar
1 teaspoon salt
Confectioners' sugar to taste

*Almost any soufflé
(including this
one) can be done
individually
in small ramekins,
or even in hollowed-
out orange shells,
and they behave
quite nicely.*

Butter a 2-quart straight-sided soufflé dish and sprinkle lightly with
a small amount of sugar; set aside. Preheat the oven to 450 degrees.
Combine the egg yolks and 2/3 cup sugar in a double boiler. Cook until
the mixture is thick and begins to coat a spoon, whisking constantly.
Add the liqueur. Whisk constantly until the custard is once again warm.
Do not allow it to curdle.

Beat the egg whites, cream of tartar, and salt in a mixer bowl until the
egg whites mound but do not break apart. If they do break apart from
overbeating, beat in 1 more egg white.

Fold a small amount of the egg whites into the egg yolks; fold the egg
yolks into the egg whites. Be careful to keep the whites from deflating.
Spoon into the prepared soufflé dish.

Place the soufflé in the oven, and immediately reduce the oven
temperature to 425 degrees. Bake for about 25 to 30 minutes or until
the soufflé has risen and a knife inserted near the center comes out
clean. Remove from the oven, and sprinkle with confectioners' sugar.
Serve immediately.

Serves 6

The most important thing to remember with any quick bread or cookie or muffin is to not overhandle them. If they are rough in appearance, they taste better. When I ran a bakery/restaurant/catering business in the 1980s, we used an ice cream scoop for the cookies and muffins, and we barely worked the gingerbread-man-dough to keep it moist and almost sticky. Also, we made our cookies, gingerbread men, scones, and muffins big. There again, the larger any of them are, the better they taste. Occasionally people would ask us to make small cocktail-size or tea-size cookies or even small tea breads for parties. We would do these rather reluctantly, because the smaller items never baked right.

Cookies and "pick-up" desserts eaten out of hand bake best on shiny cookie sheets. If yours are dull and thin, use two thin cookie sheets together as one, and line the top one with shiny foil. Then the cookies and desserts will bake without getting hard or without burning on the bottom. Remove them from the oven while they are still a little soft in the middle. This is especially important with gingerbread men, because they will continue to bake on the hot cookie sheets after they are removed from the oven.

If some seem particularly under-done but do not need to go back into the oven, leave them on the hot cookie sheets to cool down, and they will continue to bake. For "pick-up" desserts, a long, slow oven temperature bakes a lot nicer product than a hot, high oven temperature does. Anything that has brown sugar, molasses, and/or honey will especially need a lower temperature for a longer bake since they tend to burn rather easily. Let the cookies or whatever cool to room temperature before eating them, because, as with all baking, it takes them a while to "settle down" (and also, if you don't, you'll burn your tongue off).

Baking Cookies & Things

To Eat Out of Hand

Contents

Sugar Cookies

For years I have looked for a really good sugar cookie recipe to use for decorating for the holidays. I wanted one that keeps its white-sugary look and stays soft after it is baked. Finally, at one of our church dinners, I found the cookie. It was a real treasure hunt to search out the baker, who turned out to be Elizabeth House, a young girl in our congregation. About two days later, she sent me the recipe in the mail, neatly typed in red and green Christmas ink. Thank you, Elizabeth; you obviously have a lot of love to give, and I thank you for sharing it with me.

5 cups all-purpose flour
1 1/2 teaspoons baking powder
1 teaspoon salt
1/2 teaspoon baking soda
1 cup (2 sticks) unsalted butter, softened
2/3 cup vegetable shortening
2 cups sugar
2/3 cup sour cream
2 eggs, beaten
2 teaspoons vanilla extract
1 teaspoon almond, lemon, or orange flavoring (optional)
4 cups (or more) confectioners' sugar
1/4 cup milk

Mix the flour, baking powder, salt, and baking soda together. Cream the butter, shortening, and sugar in a mixer bowl for 6 to 8 minutes or until light and fluffy. Add the sour cream, eggs, vanilla, and almond flavoring, mixing well and scraping the side of the bowl occasionally. Add the flour mixture gradually, beating well after each addition; do not overbeat.

Roll the dough 1/4 inch thick on a lightly floured surface. Cut into desired shapes, and place on a lightly oiled foil-lined cookie sheet. Bake at 350 degrees for 7 to 8 minutes or until lightly browned.

Sift the confectioners' sugar into a bowl. Add the milk gradually, mixing until smooth. It should not be too thin; add more confectioners' sugar if needed. Spread over the warm cookies.

Makes about 2 dozen large cookies

If you are at all artistic, these Sugar Cookies make perfect "sand dollars," like you find at the beach. I mound these up into little pyramids, and pencil in the sand dollar markings.

These cookies stay white even after they bake, so they make very nice sand dollars or most other shaped cookies.

Chocolate Chip Cookies

This makes a very big batch of cookies, but the dough can be frozen for up to six weeks. The original recipe was this recipe times four, which could only be mixed with a commercial mixer. This amount will work with a large heavy-duty mixer such as a Hobart or KitchenAid K-5.

We baked these in triple batches right up to the very minute we closed the doors of our restaurant, and we sold every one of them. Should you not want cookies all over the place, you can halve this recipe. Sometimes we need a big batch, though, and since these are drop cookies, they are easy to make and bake.

2 cups (4 sticks) unsalted butter, softened
1 cup packed brown sugar
1 cup sugar
4 eggs, beaten
6 cups all-purpose flour
2 teaspoons salt
2 teaspoons baking soda
1 cup pecan pieces
4 cups chocolate chips
1 tablespoon vanilla extract

The final recipe for these cookies came from our "testing committee," when I ran a bakery/ restaurant/cooking school/catering business. Tom Harris and our chef, Sharon Campbell, came up with the winning recipes. Since it was a tie, we combined the two recipes. They were very popular.

Cream the butter, brown sugar, and sugar in a mixer bowl for 8 minutes or until light and fluffy. You cannot over-cream this. Add the eggs one at a time, beating well after each addition and scraping the bowl occasionally. Add the flour, salt, and baking soda, and mix well. Add the pecans, chocolate chips, and vanilla. Mix well, but do not overbeat.

Shape into golf ball-size (or larger) cookies, and place 1 inch apart on a well-oiled foil-lined cookie sheet. Bake at 325 degrees for about 6 to 8 minutes or until lightly browned. Do not overbake; these will continue cooking after you take them out of the oven. Cool on a wire rack.

Makes 4 dozen or more very large cookies

Gingerbread Men

This could be gingerbread people, because it makes a wonderful dough to cut out in any shapes, men or women, boys or girls. I prefer large shapes to smaller ones, because the smaller ones bake too hard. There are myriad cookie cutters out there, in all kinds of wonderfully imaginative shapes. I have listed some of the companies that carry them on pages 170–171 under Sources.

7 to 8 cups all-purpose flour
1 tablespoon baking soda
2 teaspoons salt
2 teaspoons ginger
1 teaspoon ground cloves
1 teaspoon freshly ground allspice
1 teaspoon freshly ground cinnamon

1 teaspoon freshly ground nutmeg
1 cup (2 sticks) unsalted butter, softened
1 cup packed dark brown sugar
1 1/2 cups dark molasses (not blackstrap)
3 eggs, beaten

Sift the flour, baking soda, salt, ginger, cloves, allspice, cinnamon, and nutmeg together. Beat the butter and brown sugar in a mixer bowl until blended and smooth. Add the molasses and eggs, and beat until light and fluffy. Add the flour mixture gradually, beating at low speed just until mixed. Do not overbeat.

Cut the dough into 2 large pieces. Wrap 1 in plastic wrap, and place it in the refrigerator. Pat the remaining dough into an oval about 1/2 inch thick on a lightly floured surface. Roll the dough into a smooth, even oval. Cut the dough into the desired shapes, and place them on a lightly oiled shiny cookie sheet (or you can use a Silpat sheet or other commercial sheet).

Bake at 325 degrees for 8 to 10 minutes or until almost done. The centers should be a little damp and not completely set; they will continue to cook on the hot cookie sheet. If you have left them in the oven too long, use a spatula to remove them at once from the hot cookie sheet to a wire rack.

Repeat the process with the remaining dough. You can instead keep the remaining dough chilled for several days or frozen for up to 2 months. Just don't allow it to dry out; keep it tightly wrapped.

Makes 10 to 12 gingerbread people

This dough is quite easy to mix, and it keeps on hand for days. Do not overmix the dough, and do not use too much flour. The dough should be almost sticky but still easy to roll out. Too much flour, and they crack and are not pretty. It is better to err on the side of sticky.

Lemon Rounds

Lemon Squares are such a wonderful standby that there was a time when dessert tables at gatherings might contain four or five batches. These rounds make a nice change, should you encounter a plethora of the good ol' standbys at your next meeting or occasion. Rounds are a nice change of pace and are also very easy to make.

1 cup (2 sticks) unsalted butter, softened
1 cup sugar
$1/2$ teaspoon baking soda
1 teaspoon (scant) salt
Finely grated zest of 1 large lemon
$1/3$ cup fresh lemon juice
2 teaspoons vanilla extract
$2 1/3$ cups all-purpose flour
$1 1/2$ to 2 cups confectioners' sugar
2 tablespoons fresh lemon juice
2 tablespoons unsalted butter, softened

Beat 1 cup butter and the sugar in a mixer bowl until mixed. Add the baking soda, salt, lemon zest, $1/3$ cup lemon juice, and the vanilla. Beat for 1 minute or until mixed. Add the flour $1/2$ cup at a time until the mixture is thick enough to shape. You may not need all the flour.

Shape the dough into small balls. Place on a lightly oiled foil-lined cookie sheet. Bake at 350 degrees for 10 to 12 minutes. Do not let the cookies brown. Remove to a wire rack to cool.

Mix the confectioners' sugar, 2 tablespoons lemon juice, and 2 tablespoons butter in a bowl. Spread or brush over each cookie.

Makes about 3 dozen small cookies

Peanut Butter Cookies

The third most popular cookie we made in our restaurant/bakery business during the 1980s was this peanut butter cookie. The most popular was the chocolate chip cookie, then the Heath bar cookie, then these. Scones were the most popular "out of hand" item, but they differ somewhat from actual cookies.

This recipe makes 8 dozen small cookies, but we never made small ones. Ours were huge, thick, and chewy. I think small cookies get too hard in baking regardless of how you cut down the baking time. If you make large ones with this recipe, you will still get about 4 dozen. You can freeze the dough for later use if you get tired of juggling all those cookie sheets.

3/4 cup peanut butter
3/4 cup (1 1/2 sticks) unsalted butter, softened
1 1/2 cups sugar
1 1/2 cups packed brown sugar
3 eggs, beaten
4 cups all-purpose flour
2 teaspoons salt
1 teaspoon baking powder
1 teaspoon baking soda

Cream the peanut butter, butter, sugar, brown sugar, and eggs in a mixer bowl until light and fluffy, scraping the side of the bowl occasionally. You cannot over-cream it. Add the flour, salt, baking powder, and baking soda gradually, mixing well after each addition and scraping the bowl occasionally. Do not overbeat. Chill the dough for 4 hours to overnight.

Shape the dough into ping pong ball-size pieces. Press a criss-cross pattern into each piece with a fork. Place 1 inch apart on a lightly oiled foil-lined cookie sheet. Bake at 325 degrees for 8 to 10 minutes. Watch carefully; peanut butter burns quickly. Cool on a wire rack.

Makes 8 dozen cookies

For baking cookies and scones on a cookie sheet, I find that lightly oiled foil does the best job of baking the cookies without burning the bottom. Silpat sheets or parchment paper work well, too. The only ones that do not work for me are the very black cookie sheets. I find that a shiny pan is necessary to reflect the heat enough to bake the cookies evenly.

Basic Scones, Small Batch

4 cups all-purpose flour
1½ cups sugar
2 teaspoons salt
1 teaspoon baking soda
1 teaspoon cream of tartar
1 teaspoon cornstarch
1 cup (2 sticks) cold unsalted butter, each cut into 4 chunks
2 large eggs, beaten
1½ cups (or more) whipping cream

Combine the flour, sugar, salt, baking soda, cream of tartar, and cornstarch in a large mixer bowl. Mix with the flat beater. With the mixer running at low speed, add the cold chunks of butter. Mix until you see only small pieces of butter in the dough. Work quickly from the time you add the butter until the mixing is complete.

Add the eggs, and beat just until mixed. Add half the whipping cream, mixing quickly; do not overbeat. You may not need all the whipping cream, or you may need more depending upon the appearance and feel of the dough. It should be moist and sticky and not at all dry.

Shape the dough into balls the size of a small lemon for a rough-shaped scone; or roll or pat on a dry surface into a circle and cut into triangles. Or, as Betty Sims does in *Simply Scrumptious* (page 21), roll out and cut into heart shapes. The rolled and cut scones will be thinner than drop scones and will therefore yield more than the dropped ones.

Place the scones on a shiny heavy-duty baking sheet. (Or use two flimsier ones together; line with ungreased foil or Silpat sheets.)

Bake at 325 degrees for about 8 to 10 minutes. Baking time is long and slow, and, because of the small amount of baking soda, the scones will not brown but will begin to firm up everywhere but in their very centers. When the centers are almost firm, remove the scones from the oven to cool on the hot baking sheets. This will allow them to continue to bake. If the scones become too firm in the centers, remove them from the hot baking sheets to a cool surface.

Note: You can add 1 cup of any of the following when mixing up these scones: chocolate chips; chopped dried apricots; golden or dark raisins; toffee chips; frozen blueberries; or dried cranberries. They should be added after you work the cold butter into the dough. Be careful not to pulverize them. With soft fruit like blueberries, it is best to use them frozen.

Makes 12 to 15 drop scones, or 24 rolled scones

A sprinkling of sugar over the tops of the hot scones, fresh from the oven, makes them really delicious.

For Chocolate Chip Scones, glaze with a mixture of 1 cup confectioners' sugar, grated zest of 1 large orange, and ¼ cup fresh orange juice. (You may need a bit more or less confectioners' sugar to make a thick glaze that will stick to the hot scones.)

For Citrus Scones (or other Fruit Scones), substitute lemon juice for the orange juice and lemon zest for the orange zest. Lemon glaze is especially delicious on blueberry scones, but to keep the blueberries from becoming mush, use them frozen, even if you bought them fresh. They mix and bake better frozen.

"*Small*" *is relative here. If you are using a 5-quart mixer (which most KitchenAid and Hobart mixers are), the small batch will be a regular size batch for you. A 4-quart or smaller mixer will make it seem like a huge batch, and it might even burn out the motor on your machine. Check your manufacturer's product description for the maximum capacity of your mixer. Divide the recipe exactly by two if your mixer's capacity is smaller than 4 quarts.*

Oddly enough, the larger the batch, the better the scones taste. I'm sure my friends Rose Berenbaum and Shirley Corriher could tell us exactly why this is, chemically, and I fully intend to ask them someday. However, first things first. Because leavening agents such as baking soda and baking powder generally begin their work the instant they are mixed with a liquid, the leavening with quick breads begins to change if it sits there unbaked for too long. The dough has behaved rather nicely for me, however, when, out of necessity, I have had to shape the scones from the raw mixed dough, freeze the unbaked scones on a baking sheet, then bake them later, from either the frozen or thawed state. In fact, I like the scones better that way. That'll go on my "Rose and Shirley List of Questions."

For Apricot Scones or Dried Cherry Scones, melt 1 cup chocolate chips with 1 tablespoon unsalted butter. Mix with 1 tablespoon vanilla extract and 1/4 cup boiling water to make a smooth paste. If the chocolate seizes and looks awful, add more boiling water 1 tablespoon at a time to relax the chocolate paste; it will become smooth. (Do not try this with expensive chocolate—unlike grocery store brand chocolate chips, expensive chocolate needs to be tempered, and you don't want to do that just for a little chocolate glaze over a scone or two. If you really, really do want to use Vahlrona or some such finer chocolate, please refer to Sources, page 170. There are a number of excellent books on the subject of tempering chocolate.)

Gingerbread Scones

The addition of chopped crystallized (or candied) ginger that you find with the spices or oriental foods at the grocery store adds a lot of zing to these scones. Chop the ginger with a knife, because a processor makes it too sticky to use in the batter. Fresh gingerroot can be grated to add a much more pungent flavor than the crystallized ginger, and the fresh, of course, makes the scones much less sweet than the crystallized. Grate fresh gingerroot across the grain into the bowl, so that you catch all its juices. Grating across the grain keeps it from becoming too fibrous to eat.

3 cups all-purpose flour
1 cup quick-cooking (not instant) oats
1 cup packed dark brown sugar
2 teaspoons salt
1 teaspoon baking powder
1 teaspoon cream of tartar
1 teaspoon cornstarch
2 teaspoons dried ginger
2 teaspoons cinnamon
2 teaspoons nutmeg
3 tablespoons chopped crystallized ginger, or 2 tablespoons grated fresh gingerroot

$1/2$ cup (1 stick) unsalted butter, softened
2 teaspoons vanilla extract
2 eggs, beaten
$1/4$ cup dark molasses (not unsulfured)
$1/4$ to $1/2$ cup heavy cream
3 tablespoons unsalted butter
$1/4$ cup sugar

Combine the flour, oats, brown sugar, salt, baking powder, cream of tartar, cornstarch, dried ginger, cinnamon, nutmeg, and crystallized ginger in a large mixer bowl. Beat at low speed until mixed. Add $1/2$ cup butter 1 tablespoon at a time, beating until the butter is the size of peas. Do not overbeat.

Combine the vanilla, eggs, and molasses in a bowl, and mix well. Add to the flour mixture, beating at very low speed just until mixed. The dough should barely be moist. Add the cream gradually, mixing until the dough is wet but can still be handled.

Use a $1/4$ cup dry measuring cup to scoop out the dough. Place each scoop on a lightly oiled foil-lined baking sheet. Bake at 350 degrees for about 20 minutes or until all the scones are done. Do not overbake.

Rub 3 tablespoons butter over the tops of the hot scones. Sprinkle with $1/4$ cup sugar.

Makes 12 to 15 scones

Lemon Poppy Seed Scones

You can substitute sesame seeds for the poppy seeds if you prefer. Sesame seeds have a nicer flavor if they are lightly toasted. Simply spread the sesame seeds on a lightly oiled foil-lined baking sheet, and bake at 350 degrees for about 6 minutes; stir them once or twice. Those little seeds would just as soon burn as look at you, so you'd better keep an eye on them. You can brown them with a tiny bit of oil in a large skillet, but they jump all over the place when you do, so I think the oven is easier. There is no need to toast poppy seeds.

Grated zest of 2 large lemons
$1/4$ cup poppy seeds
3 cups all-purpose flour
1 cup sugar
1 teaspoon baking soda
1 teaspoon cream of tartar
1 teaspoon cornstarch
2 teaspoons salt
$3/4$ cup ($1^{1}/2$ sticks) unsalted butter, softened
Juice of 2 large lemons
Milk
2 eggs, beaten
$1/2$ cup (or more) heavy cream
2 cups confectioners' sugar
2 tablespoons lemon juice

Mix the lemon zest and poppy seeds together. Set aside. Combine the flour, sugar, baking soda, cream of tartar, cornstarch, and salt in a large mixer bowl. Beat at low speed until blended and smooth. Add the poppy seed mixture, and mix well. With the mixer running at low speed, add the butter a few tablespoons at a time, mixing until the butter is visible as pea-size chunks.

Mix the juice of 2 lemons with enough milk to measure $1/2$ cup. Combine with the eggs and cream in a bowl. Add to the flour mixture and mix well, scraping the side of the bowl occasionally. If the mixture is very dry, add additional cream 1 tablespoon at a time until the batter can be scooped up.

Scoop up $1/4$ cup of the batter for each scone, and place on a lightly oiled baking sheet. Bake at 375 degrees for 15 to 20 minutes or until the center scone is done. Combine the confectioners' sugar and 2 tablespoons lemon juice in a bowl, mixing until a smooth paste forms. Let stand for 5 minutes or longer. Glaze each scone with about 2 tablespoons of the mixture.

Makes 12 to 14 large scones

Whenever you are using any kind of oily seeds, such as sesame seeds or poppy seeds, be sure that the oil they contain has not turned rancid. Keeping them in the refrigerator can prevent this, but if you don't use a lot of seeds in cooking, be sure to date their little bottles or cans. They don't keep much longer than four or five months refrigerated. (Pecans and almost all nuts turn rancid very quickly, and they should be frozen to prevent this.)

Oatmeal Raisin Scones

The same basic rules for scones apply to these as well: no baking powder, quick mixing, moist dough, minimum handling, and avoiding overbaking. You can substitute any other dried fruit for the raisins. Dark raisins, chopped dried apricots, or 1 large fresh peeled and chopped apple, or a combination of any of these fruits makes delicious scones with a wonderful texture to offset the rather bulky oats. My favorite fruits for scones are mixed dried "tropical mixture," but any combination is good.

3 cups all-purpose flour
1 cup rolled oats (not instant)
$1/2$ cup packed light brown sugar
$1/2$ cup sugar
2 teaspoons salt
1 teaspoon baking soda
1 teaspoon cream of tartar
1 teaspoon cornstarch
1 teaspoon cinnamon
1 teaspoon nutmeg
2 teaspoons vanilla extract
$3/4$ cup cream
$1/4$ cup vegetable oil
2 eggs, beaten
1 cup golden raisins
2 cups confectioners' sugar (optional)
2 tablespoons orange juice (optional)

Combine the flour, oats, brown sugar, sugar, salt, baking soda, cream of tartar, cornstarch, cinnamon, and nutmeg in a mixer bowl, and mix well.

Mix the vanilla, cream, vegetable oil, and eggs in a bowl. With the mixer running at low speed, add to the flour mixture, scraping the side of the bowl occasionally. Add the raisins, and mix quickly.

Shape into large scones, and place on a lightly oiled baking sheet. Bake at 375 degrees for 15 to 20 minutes or until the center scone tests done. Let stand until cool.

Combine the confectioners' sugar with the orange juice in a bowl, mixing until a smooth paste forms. Spoon 1 to 2 tablespoons over each scone. If you prefer, you can omit the glaze and sprinkle each scone with additional sugar or confectioners' sugar.

Makes 12 to 14 large scones

Brown Sugar Pecan Scones

You can add toffee pieces (or "brickle") to these if your diet and conscience allow. The scones are a lot sweeter that way, but the pecans balance it out nicely.

4 cups all-purpose flour
1/2 cup packed dark brown sugar
1/4 cup sugar
2 teaspoons salt
2 teaspoons cinnamon
2 teaspoons nutmeg
2 teaspoons cardamom
1 teaspoon baking soda
1 teaspoon cream of tartar
1 teaspoon cornstarch
2 teaspoons vanilla extract
3/4 cup milk
1/4 cup vegetable oil
2 eggs, beaten
1 1/2 cups chopped pecans
1 cup toffee pieces (optional)
1 cup packed dark brown sugar
2 tablespoons (or more) hot apple juice

Combine the flour, 1/2 cup brown sugar, sugar, salt, cinnamon, nutmeg, cardamom, baking soda, cream of tartar, and cornstarch in a large mixer bowl. Beat at low speed until mixed well.

Mix the vanilla, milk, vegetable oil, and eggs in a bowl. With the mixer running at low speed, add to the flour mixture. Mix well, but do not overbeat. Fold in the pecans and toffee pieces.

Scoop up 1/4 cup of the batter for each scone, and place on a lightly oiled foil-lined baking sheet. Bake at 350 degrees for 18 to 20 minutes or until the center scone tests done. Do not overbake.

Combine 1 cup brown sugar with the apple juice in a bowl, stirring until the brown sugar is dissolved and the mixture is the consistency of a stiff syrup. Add a small amount of additional juice if needed. Spoon over the cooled scones.

Makes 12 to 15 large scones

Bloody Mary Scones

Scones that are not sweet (that is, "savory") are wonderful accompaniments to spicy Bloody Mary-type drinks, at morning meetings with coffee or tea, and especially at teatime. The lack of sugar in the scones adds a nice change to a simple little fluffy "not-cookie."

3¹/2 cups all-purpose flour
1 tablespoon salt
1 teaspoon baking soda
1 teaspoon cream of tartar
1 teaspoon cornstarch
1 cup (2 sticks) cold unsalted butter, cut into 8 chunks
3 large eggs, beaten
1¹/2 cups (about) V-8 juice, spicy or plain
1 cup shredded sharp Cheddar cheese
1 cup chopped green olives (optional)
¹/2 cup plain Rice Krispies (optional)

Use your imagination to come up with your own savory scones. (The base line of flour, three leavening agents, eggs, and butter is a constant.) You can even substitute V-8 juice or tomato juice for the milk for a very spicy scone, or half chocolate milk and half very strong coffee for mocha scones. I glaze the mocha ones with a chocolate glaze. They are great with coffee or lattes or even with plain milk.

Combine the flour, salt, baking soda, cream of tartar, and cornstarch in a large mixer bowl. Beat with the flat beater until well mixed. With the mixer running at low speed, add the butter. Mix until the butter is visible as pea-size pieces. Work quickly from the time you add the butter until the mixing is complete. Add the eggs, mixing quickly.

Add half the V-8 juice at a time, mixing quickly after each addition. You may need more or less juice depending on the appearance and feel of the dough. It should be quite moist, but not too sticky to handle and not at all dry. Do not overmix, or the scones will be tough. Fold in the cheese, olives, and cereal.

Shape the dough into patties about the size of a lemon. Place ¹/2 inch apart on a lightly oiled baking sheet. Bake at 325 degrees for about 8 to 10 minutes or until the center scone is firm to the touch when pressed.

Cool on the baking sheet for about 5 minutes. Remove to a wire rack to cool completely.

Makes 12 to 15 large scones

Chèvre and Green Onion Scones

Laura Chenel in California is rightfully credited with the "chèvre revolution" back in the early 1980s. I reported on an Entrepreneurs Seminar for a publication several years ago, in which Laura, Chuck Williams (of Williams-Sonoma), Paula Lambert (of The Mozzarella Co., Inc.), and Bruce Aidells (of sausage fame) explained how they became successful entrepreneurs. Having been dubbed one myself many years ago by The Birmingham News, *I wondered why they showed no signs of weariness. None of them had lost their zeal, their love, or their passion for what they were doing.*

Thanks, Laura, and all of you for your gentle love and persistence. You still inspire worn-out retired former entrepreneurs like me.

4 cups all-purpose flour
2 teaspoons salt
1 teaspoon baking soda
1 teaspoon cream of tartar
1 teaspoon cornstarch
1 teaspoon freshly ground pepper
1 cup (2 sticks) cold unsalted butter, cut into 8 chunks

8 ounces plain or herbed goat cheese (without ashes)
4 large eggs, beaten
1 cup buttermilk
1/2 cup (about) heavy cream or milk
3 green onions, chopped, with some of the green included

Combine the flour, salt, baking soda, cream of tartar, cornstarch, and pepper in a large mixer bowl. Beat with the flat beater until well mixed. With the mixer running at low speed, add the chunks of butter. Mix until the butter is visible as pea-size pieces. Work quickly from the time you add the butter until the mixing is complete.

Fold in the goat cheese gradually. You should still see lumps of it when all of it has been added. Add the eggs, beating just until mixed. Add the buttermilk and half the cream quickly. You may need more or less cream, depending on the appearance and feel of the dough. It should be quite moist but not too sticky to handle and not at all dry. Fold in the green onions. Be sure they are well distributed.

Shape the dough into patties about the size of a lemon. Place 1/2 inch apart on a lightly oiled foil-lined baking sheet. Bake at 350 degrees for 10 to 12 minutes or until the center scone tests done.

Makes 12 to 15 very large scones, or 24 medium scones

Laura's comments have echoed through my head for years now. She got into the goat cheese business, she said, because she "loved the little creatures, and wanted them to earn their keep." Her advice to others was, "Please find a creature to love who has a larger 'container' than little goats do. Cows, too, can produce lovely cheeses."

Bran Muffins

When I had my restaurant and bakery, we made 14 dozen of these muffins every single morning all year long. During the holidays, we were too busy to count how many batches we made, but by the end of every day they were all sold. Like the scones and the cookies, I think I can still make these blindfolded. I know that back in those years I made them most mornings with my eyes closed.

We scooped them out into lightly oiled muffin papers in the big commercial muffin cups with a medium-size ice cream scoop. Too much batter, and they overflow; too little, and they burn because of all the dark brown sugar and molasses. Fill your paper muffin liners a good 2/3 full.

This batter does not like to sit overnight as some batters do, because the baking soda deactivates after a while and the muffins are flat. Penny, one of my best bakers, has written on the bottom of the tattered recipe sheet from our baking book: "Makes 7 dozen. Plus one. 7-9-88."

These bran muffins freeze nicely. Evans, our youngest son, took a bag of these muffins on a two-week trip around Europe when he was 12 years old, and they kept very nicely, he said. None of the rest of us challenged him. I think that's a little long to be away from the cool safety of a refrigerator, but he loved them.

2 teaspoons baking soda
2 cups (or more) buttermilk
1 cup unsweetened plain All-Bran
1 cup golden raisins
1/4 cup (1/2 stick) unsalted butter, melted
1/2 cup dark molasses (not blackstrap)
1/4 cup honey
2 eggs, beaten
1 cup chopped pecans
2 cups unbleached whole wheat flour
2 cups unbleached white bread flour
2 teaspoons salt

Dissolve the baking soda in the buttermilk in a large bowl. Let stand for 10 minutes. Add the cereal and raisins, and mix well. Add the butter, molasses, honey, eggs, pecans, whole wheat flour, bread flour, and salt, and mix well. Sometimes the bran and/or the flour absorbs more liquid than at other times. If needed, add more buttermilk 1/2 cup at a time until the mixture is the consistency of cooked oatmeal.

Scoop out into lightly oiled paper-lined muffin cups. Bake at 375 degrees for 10 to 15 minutes or until the center muffin tests done.

Note: This dough will get tough if it is overworked, so mix this recipe by hand, not with a mixer.

Makes 2 dozen muffins (plus one)

Coconut Muffins

Coconut muffins are wonderful adjuncts to fruit salads for brunches or for afternoon teas. These muffins have a little more substance than macaroons and thus are more versatile than macaroons. The addition of 1 cup chocolate chips to the batter makes a very good and somewhat different addition to the usual tray of baked things for home or for "occasions."

You can also glaze the cooled muffins with chocolate. Melt 1 cup chocolate chips, and add 1/4 to 1/2 cup boiling water gradually to the chocolate. At some point, the chocolate will "seize," and you will have to keep adding boiling water a drop or two at a time to smooth out the mixture. Stir it with a fork to keep it smooth. A pineapple glaze is used in this recipe, but either glaze makes a wonderful treat.

2 1/2 cups all-purpose flour
1/2 cup sugar
2 teaspoons baking powder
1 teaspoon salt
1 cup flaked coconut
1 egg, beaten
2 teaspoons vanilla extract
3 tablespoons unsalted butter, melted
1 cup coconut milk (see Note)
1 cup pineapple juice or orange juice
1 tablespoon (or more) confectioners' sugar

Lightly oil paper muffin liners, and place in muffin cups. Set aside.

Combine the flour, sugar, baking powder, salt, and coconut in a large bowl, and mix well. Combine the egg, vanilla, butter, and coconut milk in a bowl, and mix until blended and smooth. Add to the flour mixture gradually, stirring just until moistened.

Fill the prepared muffin cups no more than 3/4 full. Bake at 375 degrees until each muffin tests done. Remove the muffins to a wire rack to cool.

Combine the pineapple juice and confectioners' sugar in a bowl, stirring until a smooth paste forms. Add more confectioners' sugar 1 tablespoon at a time if needed to make a thick, pourable paste. Spoon over the cooled muffins.

Note: Coconut milk is not the liquid from a fresh coconut. You can find the real coconut milk either in the bakery section of the grocery store or in the area where the bar ingredients, such as cherries and bitters, are kept.

Makes 12 muffins, or 18 miniature muffins

Gingerbread Muffins

To me, fragrant gingerbread—in the form of big, fat gingerbread boys or big, fat gingerbread girls, with raisins for eyes and buttons; or baked like a cake and then sliced and placed in a warm pool of lemon sauce; or baked as big or tiny muffins—just tends to ease my burdens.

In the winter, I keep gingerbread cookie dough rolled in fat tubes in plastic wrap and foil in the freezer ready to bake into big cookies or to roll out with the grandchildren into gingerbread boys or girls, stars, and holiday shapes. (The recipe for the cookie dough is on page 155.)

The recipe here is for the best muffins you ever tasted, if you like gingerbread like I do. Remember not to overbeat the muffin batter, even though you do have to beat cookie dough. Muffin batter should be stirred just until completely mixed, but not so much that it develops the chewing gum-like gluten of flour, which ruins muffins. Use a very thin glaze with these, rather than one that is too thick. You don't want to mask the wonderful gingery flavors.

For Citrus Honey Butter, beat 1 cup softened unsalted butter with 1/2 cup honey, the grated zest of 1 medium orange, and the grated zest of 1 very small lemon in a mixer bowl until light and fluffy. Serve with your favorite muffins.

2 cups all-purpose flour
2 teaspoons baking powder
1 teaspoon cinnamon
1 teaspoon ginger
1 teaspoon ground nutmeg
1/4 teaspoon baking soda
1 egg, beaten
3/4 cup milk
1/2 cup packed dark brown sugar

1/2 cup vegetable oil
1/4 cup dark molasses (not blackstrap)
1 cup (or more) confectioners' sugar
1/4 cup undiluted frozen apple juice concentrate, or 1/4 cup bourbon, or a combination of the two

Lightly oil paper muffin liners, and place them in muffin cups. Set aside. Mix the flour, baking powder, cinnamon, ginger, nutmeg, and baking soda in a large bowl. Mix the egg, milk, brown sugar, vegetable oil, and molasses in a bowl. Add to the flour mixture, stirring just until mixed. The batter should be somewhat lumpy.

Fill the prepared muffin cups 2/3 full. Bake at 375 degrees for 25 minutes or until a wooden pick inserted in the center muffin comes out clean. Remove from the muffin cups, and cool on a wire rack.

Combine the confectioners' sugar and apple juice in a bowl, stirring with a fork just until smooth. The glaze should be thin. Add more confectioners' sugar if needed.

Note: Catalogues seem to come in hordes in our mail these days, and the baking ones are astounding. Look for pretty shapes for these and other muffins. These gingerbread muffins are beautiful baked in deep heart-shaped muffin tins. I have listed in Sources some of the companies that carry these lovely baking utensils.

Makes 12 medium muffins

Doughnuts

There is probably nothing more wonderful to me than a plate of
homemade doughnuts. You have to admit that they are a very rare
commodity. As we age, we tend to abandon doughnuts altogether, for
calorie or cholesterol reasons. That is a shame, because doughnuts are a
real treat. Homemade doughnuts are easy, but they certainly don't look like
it. In the fall of the year, they are wonderful with hot apple cider, or with
coffee all year round. You do need a doughnut cutter, if you are going to be
traditional, although square doughnuts are just as good as the round ones.
Cut them about 2 inches square, and bake them like the traditional ones.

2 tablespoons yeast
1 cup milk, warmed to about
    100 degrees
2 teaspoons sugar
2 teaspoons salt
1 1/2 cups all-purpose flour
1 cup packed brown sugar
2 cups all-purpose flour
1/4 cup vegetable oil

1 tablespoon vanilla extract
2 eggs, beaten
1 teaspoon freshly grated nutmeg
Grated zest of 1 small lemon
1 tablespoon unsalted butter,
    melted
Confectioners' sugar
Sugar to taste

These are baked yeast-risen doughnuts. They can be fried in oil instead of being baked in the oven, but the baked ones are completely different in taste. You can add any of the following to the batter before the second rise: 1 cup miniature chocolate chips; 3 tablespoons grated orange zest; 1 cup sweetened coconut; or even 1 cup chopped nuts. You can glaze them with the Chocolate Glaze from page 139 if you like. Pour the glaze over the cooled doughnuts. All small yeast breads dry out rather quickly, so keep the baked doughnuts covered. I invert a large metal mixing bowl over the platter until serving time.

Combine the yeast, milk, and 2 teaspoons sugar in a large mixer bowl,
stirring until the yeast and sugar are dissolved. Add the salt and 1 1/2
cups flour, and beat until mixed. Let rise, covered with a warm cloth, for
about 1 hour or until doubled in bulk.

Combine the brown sugar, 2 cups flour, the vegetable oil, vanilla, eggs,
nutmeg, and lemon zest in a food processor, and process until smooth.
(If your brown sugar was hard, this will smooth it out.) The batter
should be very smooth.

Punch down the dough in the mixer bowl. Add the brown sugar mixture,
beating until mixed and scraping the side of the bowl occasionally. Let
rise for about 1 hour or until doubled in bulk.

Punch down the dough again. Spread on a floured surface, and roll
into an oval 1/2 inch thick. Cut out with a doughnut cutter. Rework any
leftover dough. (The dough is sticky, and the flour on the surface will
help you roll and cut it better; but do not use so much flour that the
dough dries out.) Place the doughnuts 2 inches apart on a lightly oiled
baking sheet. Let rise for 30 minutes or until doubled in bulk. Brush
with some of the melted butter. Bake at 400 degrees for 8 to 10 minutes
or until golden brown. Brush with the remaining melted butter. Sprinkle
the hot doughnuts with confectioners' sugar and additional sugar.

Makes 18 doughnuts

Sources

Cake Supplies

Maid of Scandinavia
P.O. Box 39426
Edina, MN 55439
Catalogue upon request:
cake supplies, baking and
decorating supplies, some
chocolates

Wilton Enterprises
2240 West 75th Street
Woodbridge, IL 60517
Fax: (630) 963-7299

Cheeses

Laura Chenel's Chèvre Inc.
4310 Fremont Drive
Sonoma, CA 95476
Fax: (707) 996-1816
Fresh goat cheeses

Mozzarella Company
2944 Elm Street
Dallas, TX 75226
Fax: (214) 741-4076
Website: www.mozzco.com
e-mail: mozzco@aol
Wonderful hand-crafted
cheeses; catalogue; fast
shipping

Cherries

Cherry Marketing Institute
P.O. Box 30285
Lansing, MI 48909-7785
Fax: (517) 669-3354
e-mail: jbaker@cherrymkt.org

Chukar Cherries Company
P.O. Box 510
320 Wine Country Road
Prosser, WA 99350
Website: www.chukar.com
Produces dried cherries and
whole fruit fillings and
sauces

Chocolate

Hershey Foods Corporation
14 E. Chocolate Avenue
Hershey, PA 17033
Fax: (717) 534-7268
Website: www.hersheys.com

Nestle Canada
25 Sheppard Avenue, W.
North York, ON Canada
M2N 6S8
Fax: (416) 218-2739

Vahlrona Chocolate. *See*
Williams-Sonoma

Facts about Chocolate; Tempering; etc.

Corriher, Shirley. 1996. *Cookwise*.
William Morrow and
Company, Inc;
pages 458, ff.

Gonzalez, Elaine. 1983. *Chocolate
Artistry*. Chicago:
Contemporary Books, Inc.

Kitchen Supplies, Bakeware, etc. *See also* Wilton; Maid of Scandinavia

Martha Stewart
Phone: (800) 950-7130
Website:
  www.marthabymail.com
Beautiful bakeware, cookie
  cutters, decorating supplies

Sur La Table
1806 Fourth Street
Berkeley, CA 94710
Fax: (510) 849-1980
Website: www.surlatable.com
Catalogue: bakeware, etc.

Williams-Sonoma
Phone: (877) 812-6235
Fax: (702) 363-2541
Website: www.williams-
  sonoma.com
Baking supplies of every kind

Lamb
Jamison Farm
171 Jamison Lane
Latrobe, PA 15650
Website: www.jamisonfarm.com

Miscellaneous Meats
Aidells Sausage
618 Coventry Road
Kensington, CA 94707
Fax: (510) 526-1116
Website: www.aidells.com

Nueske-Hillcrest Farm Meats
RR 2, P.O. Box D
Wittenberg, WI 54499
Fax: (715) 253-2021
Website: www.nueske.com
Catalogue upon request:
  wonderful bacon, etc.

Tangerines
Honey Bell Tangerines @ Mack's
  Groves
Phone: (800) 327-3525
Website: www.macks-groves.com
Incredibly delicious Indian
  River (FL) fruit. Cannot ship
  to certain states.

Other
Curl, Michael. 1982.
  The Wordsmith Dictionary
  of Anagrams. Wordswords
  Editions, Ltd.
  ISBN: 1-85326-350-8

Esquivel, Laura. 1994. *Like*
  Water for Chocolate. Vintage
  Anchor Publishing.
  ISBN: 0385-471-483

Sims, Betty. 1997. *Southern*
  Scrumptious: How to Cater
  Your Own Party. FRP.
  ISBN: 0-9659053-0-6

Index

Baking Secrets

Bonnie Bailey / L&B Vero
127 Queensberry Crescent • Birmingham, Alabama 35223

Please send _____ copies of *Baking Secrets* at $19.95 each $ _____

Add postage and handling at $3.00 each $ _____

Alabama residents add sales tax at $1.52 each $ _____

Total $ _____

Name _____

Address _____

City _____ State _____ Zip _____

Telephone _____

For volume purchases, call (205) 970-0550.
Please make checks payable to Bonnie Bailey.

Baking Secrets

Bonnie Bailey / L&B Vero
127 Queensberry Crescent • Birmingham, Alabama 35223

Please send _____ copies of *Baking Secrets* at $19.95 each $ _____

Add postage and handling at $3.00 each $ _____

Alabama residents add sales tax at $1.52 each $ _____

Total $ _____

Name _____

Address _____

City _____ State _____ Zip _____

Telephone _____

For volume purchases, call (205) 970-0550.
Please make checks payable to Bonnie Bailey.

Photocopies will be accepted.